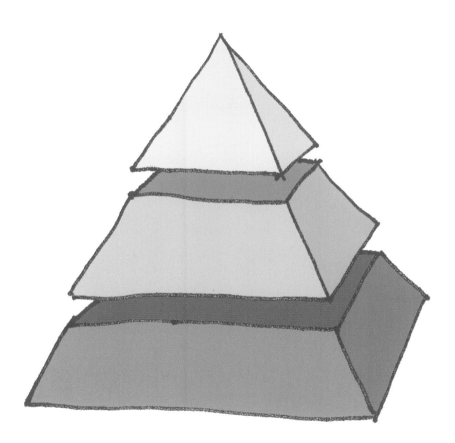

DO IT RIGHT

A CEO's Guide to
Web Strategy

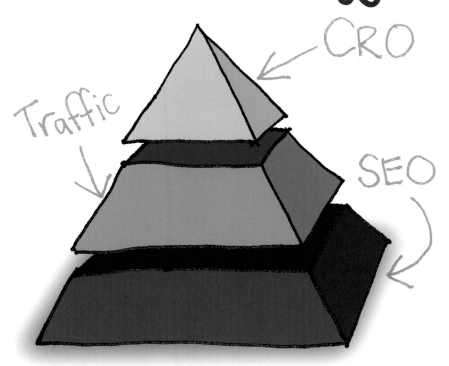

Corey A. Smith

Do It Right: A CEO's Guide to Web Strategy
By Corey Smith

Copyright © 2011
ISBN: 978-1-61206-020-0

Cover and Interior Design by Andy Harl
Graphics and Illustrations by Don Elliott

AlohaPublishing.com

First Edition, 2011

Printed in the United States of America

Contents

WEB MARKETING   83

WRAPPING IT UP   119

THE SMITHS

This book is dedicated to my beautiful bride, Jennifer and my five wonderful children, Benjamin, Bethany, Hyrum, Jenna and Ian. Without their willingness to put up with "just one more project," this book never would have happened.

SIDEBAR LEGEND

From the Blogs

Sometimes it's A.D.D. and sometimes it's relevant. When I have a specific point to make, I write a little blog post. Instead of making you go to my website, you get to read them here.

Definition

Certain terms are more important than others. I've called them out to clarify some terms for you.

Book

I like reading books and I think there is value in what other authors have to say… even if I don't agree with them. These are book recommendations for you.

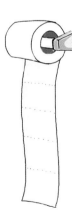

BS Meter

As a CEO, you need a BS meter to help prevent you from making a wrong choice. In some cases, there are very specific things people say that you'll need to watch for… so I've called them out. The higher on the BS meter (e.g. 4/5 or 5/5) the more you need to watch what else that person might say.

How It Starts

In February 2011, I taught an eCommerce class, which was designed as a high-level introduction to the subject. I deal with this every day and have found some key ways to teach my clients about how it works. In transferring this real-world experience to the classroom, my aim was to make eCommerce accessible to these young business students. My hope was that they would feel confident in helping to manage Web marketing projects in the future.

I received a curriculum that was, at best, okay. When I received the class textbook, I started reading it, wanting to make sure that it made sense for my students. When I woke up 20 minutes later, I realized that I hadn't turned the page.

Now, I understand that the first real issue is the fact that textbooks suck. I think that, by definition, they are required to suck. Textbooks are too long, too hard to understand and try to teach too much information, most of which students will honestly never need. Often, the instructors assigned to teach these courses have very little real experience with the subject matter.

What made the textbook an even greater problem was that an accounting and information systems professor from an obscure university in New England wrote it. The textbook was full of boring, impractical and almost useless information—the very same information that would later affect students' choices in the workplace.

It had hardly any useful tools to help students understand the marketing process and each person's role.

This leads to the real issue: the importance of eCommerce decision-making is misunderstood. Too many people think that online marketing is an IT decision, an accounting decision or a marketing decision.

They are wrong.

Just like all marketing endeavors, eCommerce should be a business decision. The marketer's job is to build the strategy to "sell" the business. The IT people make the business work technically, but should never decide on any business elements. The accounting people need to analyze how everything will be paid for.

> All men can see these tactics whereby I conquer, but what none can see is the strategy out of which victory is evolved.
> - Sun Tzu

So, why the misconception? I don't know why it didn't occur to me before this, but most Web books are not written for business leaders. They are written for the coder, marketer, IT professional or designer. There are a few great books about the Web for business leaders, and they are mentioned throughout this book as recommended readings. Still, most of the instruction regarding online marketing is aimed at these other roles—none of which should be making key, strategic business decisions.

Because these books are written for the non-business audience, students end up spending way too much time learning tools that are only valid for a year or two at most. Often, even by graduation time, the students' knowledge is becoming obsolete.

This is why I wrote this book. Unlike most of the books out there, this book is written from a strategic perspective. Yes, there are some details, but we aren't going to waste time on which Web browser you should be using, which server makes the most sense for your project or which coding language is right. We won't be spending time on the building of your website, except to understand how it fits into the bigger picture.

This book will help you understand what decisions to make and how to best make those decisions. The most important thing you should get out of this book is an effective BS meter. You'll know when someone is blowing smoke and when someone is helping you make an effective business decision.

This book is about strategic thinking; it will help you understand what is possible and what should be considered. As a CEO, it's your job to make sure that your business objectives are met strategically... not try to figure out how to put all the puzzle pieces together.

Methodology

REMEMBER VIN FIZZ?

In 1911, newspaper publisher William Randolph Hearst made an offer of $50,000 to the first person that could fly a plane from New York to LA in under 30 consecutive days. Calbraith "Cal" Perry Rodgers took up the challenge.

Of course, Cal didn't have any money. He had the plane, but in the "good ole days" an airplane required a very large support crew. So, he started talking to businesses about possible sponsorships and was able to secure a sponsorship from Armour and Company for the 1911 Wright Flyer. The company had created a new grape soft drink called Vin Fiz and wanted to get the word out.

The Vin Fiz Flyer was born. Emblazoned with the logo for Vin Fiz and messages of "Drink Vin Fiz" and "Ideal Grape Drink," Cal began his journey across North America, beginning from Sheepshead Bay, New York on September 17, 1911. Not to be outdone, all of the support train cars, paid for by Armor and Company, also sported messages of "Drink Vin Fiz."

Of course, none of this changed the fact that the grape soda, advertised as the "Sparkling Grape Drink" did not even come close to living up to its purported luster.

People described the joy of drinking Vin Fiz:

"Tastes like a cross between river water (sludge) and horse slop."

"It has a laxative effect."

And my favorite, "You have to sneak up on it to get it down."

Over the course of the next 56 days, Cal seemed to crash his way across the country more than fly. He crashed so significantly that there were very few original parts left on the plane when he finally made it to LA.

On November 12th, 1911, Cal took off from Pasadena, California in front of a crowd of some 20,000 people (all recognizing the Vin Fiz logo), but a crash in Compton gave him a concussion and a twisted spine. He spent three weeks in the hospital recovering and finally finished his journey, landing in Long Beach, California, on December 10, 1911 (54 days after he no longer qualified for the prize) with only about 82 hours spent in the air.

On top of the prestige of being the first person to fly across North America, Cal was paid $23,000 by Armour and Company for the effort. Even though he didn't win the prize of $50,000, he was at least paid well for the effort. To put that number into perspective, the median household income in 1911 was approximately $2,500.

Unfortunately, a few months later, Cal was taking a test flight in Long Beach, not far from the end of his historic flight, when he flew into a flock of seagulls and crashed into the Pacific Ocean, breaking his neck and dying. It was a sad end to an almost happy story.

You may be wondering, "What happened to Vin Fiz?"

Flock of seagulls Haircut

Well, it simply went away. The amount of money put into to launching the product and advertising the "SPARKLING Grape Drink sold at all Soda Fountains" never really took off (yeah, I get the pun). No one liked it. They all knew about it, but it tasted so bad that people didn't buy much.

100 YEAR-OLD LESSON

Search the Internet today, and you'll find website after website on the Vin Fiz Flyer. In fact, it is immortalized in the Smithsonian Air and Space Museum. Multiple books talk about the Vin Fiz Flyer, but little is said about Vin Fiz Grape Drink.

There are two lessons to learn from this story. For aviation and the Wright Brothers, this event was a spectacular success. Even for Cal, this journey was great for him and his career. Remember, Cal didn't have any money to fund his flight; he had to get help and was able to sell his vision to Armour and Company. What he did was rally people to his cause as evidenced by more than 20,000 people that were with him when he left Pasadena. This was in a time of no Internet, no text messages and no television. Cal was wildly successful, even though he fell short of his goal.

Vin Fiz, on the other hand, was a miserable failure. As this story illustrates, no amount of money spent will overcome a bad brand. No matter how much brand awareness you get, no matter how many people know about you or your business, you will never overcome the problems inherent in a bad product or service. The Vin Fiz

Groundswell by Li and Bernoff – Groundswell focuses on how businesses can take full advantage of new and emerging social platforms and technologies.

Flyer was an opportunity that would only come once. There would only be one first for a plane to go across the United States. In today's language, it was a cause that went viral. Armour and Company had some of the right elements to make their brand a huge success, namely money and visibility. The problem was that the product was bad.

Marketing is a waste of money. You don't need it.

BS Meter - 5/5

At this point, you might be thinking, "This book is supposed to be about online marketing, but you're talking about general branding and marketing. "

Let me explain.

The reality of marketing today—including online marketing—is that it is no different than it was 100 years ago. The core tenets of marketing never change. You must have a strong product and great visibility, and your business and product have to mean something to your audience. These principles make up the foundation of branding, and the Web has made the importance of doing this right even greater.

Your Web presence (website, Facebook page, etc.) allows you the opportunity to market in more ways than ever before. Your Web presence is an amplifier of who you are; it is a way to show your brand in a new, different and innovative way. If you try to hide who you are, like in the case of the Vin Fiz Grape Drink, it will only come back to haunt you. No amount of window dressing, colorful graphics or platitudes of how wonderful you are will ever mask the reality that is your brand. As the CEO, you have the opportunity to bring your brand to your client or customer in ways never thought of before—it starts with you.

While reading this book, I want to be very clear on what you should be doing. Your objective is not to fix a bad brand. You won't get any pearls of wisdom on how to create messaging on your website to overcome the challenges of your business; that is not the purpose of this book. The purpose is to help you communicate your brand message well, as well as learn how to communicate to your audience and get visibility to a level that will allow your business to catch fire...in a good way.

OLD RULES. NEW TOOLS.

Even if you are not currently on the Web with your services, your clients and prospective clients are. They are looking for you, and you may not even know it. They are talking to their friends in social media venues and searching for your services in search engines. By creating a Web presence, you invite customers to engage with you in a way that is meaningful to them.

One of the biggest challenges of online marketing is that it can be confusing and difficult to the novice. The main reason is that the Web is technical in nature.

Everyone Needs Rails

Autonomy is spectacular.

I love to do my own thing. Be a free spirit. Not conform to what other people want.

Most people want that as well. They long for the day they can go and do their own thing. They want to "fly and be free."

The problem is that most people do not function well left to their own devices. Oh sure, there are lots of people that can do that. There are entrepreneurs and creatives that can focus for hours on something and see it through to completion.

I don't think that it's about whether it's hard work or not. I don't think that is what matters. I know of plenty of people that really want to learn something new (language, sport, etc). I know of plenty of people that want to accomplish something big, create something amazing or go climb their mountain.

The problem is that with too much freedom comes too many options to consider... too many ways that you can go.

People need rails. People need constraints to guide them.

Now, the problem with the rail metaphor is that rails seem too limiting, so constricting. People think that if we are attached to rails that we can't go anywhere at all. This is simply not true.

When you think of a train, it's secured to one path, unless it meets a switch. However, trains go where the engineers tell them to go. Trains stay focused on their task at hand.

The truly inspired build their own tracks and make their own way. It's up to you to build your own tracks... your own rails to keep you focused on what you are to do.

When you get off the rails, you run the risk of not getting anywhere. So, rather than trying to jump the track and go your own way -- running the risk of running ground -- create new rails that will guide you. Create the means of staying confined to an area that makes sense. If you can't do that, find someone who can help you.

Historical methods of marketing should be rails that keep you focused in your online marketing efforts. What we are accustomed to from the past can be directly applied to today.

Most Web books talk about the history of the Web so that you, the reader, can understand how to apply it to your marketing efforts. I think that is the wrong approach to understanding online marketing, so I'm not going to waste your time talking about Al Gore's brilliant invention, the Internet, or how it has evolved over the last 20 years. It doesn't matter. The technology doesn't matter. The Internet is simply a tool to get your message out. You can look at the Vin Fiz Flyer as a great example of this. There was no email, Facebook, Twitter or YouTube that got those 20,000 people to see the Vin Fiz Flyer take off in Pasadena. It was a compelling story, and the rest took care of itself.

At the risk of sounding repetitive, I'll reiterate: when your goal is to market your business, you first need to understand that the Web is only a tool, a means to an end. If you have something that doesn't work offline, it probably won't work online. Sure, there are exceptions to the rule, but if you can't sell your product in a store, you probably can't sell it online.

Before you jump up and down saying I am wrong, let's look at an example or two. Think of the most successful websites on the Web now. The two best examples are Amazon and Facebook. Amazon simply started as an online book store. In fact, their original advertisements indicated that they were the "World's Largest Bookstore." Being online didn't change the fact that they sold books; it was just a different place for them to sell. They have now expanded their offerings to other services. Facebook, as an example, is simply an easy way for people to get together. It allows what used to be done in small groups in coffee shops, homes, parties, reunions and parks to now be done on a grand scale at home.

I know, there will always be certain examples that don't work, but they will be exceptions rather than the rule. Online marketing has nothing to do with the technology of the Web other than the fact that the tool is technical. In reality, it is the technology that seems to hang up CEOs more than anything. Concerns like, "What the hell is a

Marketing on the Web is not the same as marketing elsewhere, because the technology is different.

BS Meter – 5/5

The smaller your company is, the more likely it is that you'll need to be involved in the more specific decisions about your website. However, you'll need to be careful not to get too involved in these minute details. You do not need to understand every tool in your bag to know who should use them. Every CEO should to understand, from a high level, all the parts of the project, but should appropriately delegate. Your challenge is to know how much to keep and how much to delegate.

blog? I can't put something with that stupid of a name on my site," or, "Social media is just for 13-year-old kids and their cell phones," permeate the discussion, and I anticipate that similar complaints will abound for years to come. Online marketing uses the same philosophies and principles as marketing offline does.

There is no need to fear the technology. To understand how to build a Web presence, you don't need to know the ins and outs of intricate Web processes. You just need to take what you already know and apply it to something you're about to learn.

Think about where your business might be one year, five years or ten years from now. The way you go to market will evolve; you will evolve. Your Web presence is the easiest thing that can evolve with you. It is the simplest way to connect people with your brand in today's marketplace.

Although the thought of being responsible for a website can be daunting (and even cause heart palpitations), it doesn't have to be a scary process. Don't worry, you don't have to learn code. You don't have to learn how to use Photoshop. You don't even have to figure out the real purpose of the flux capacitor. You just have to understand enough to make sure that you are not being snookered (yeah, that's still a word). Read on, and you'll understand what your role is in the Web process.

Flux capacitor

WEB = STRATEGIC BUSINESS DECISION

Your website is a business tool and, as such, requires a business decision. Too many leaders want to abdicate responsibility in making decisions. CEOs will often defer critical decisions when they don't understand what it all means. The single most important responsibility of a CEO is ensuring that the company has a coherent message that matches the right audience.

100% of customers are people. 100% of employees are people. If you don't understand people, you don't understand business.
– Simon Sinek

When creating any marketing piece, there are four distinct roles required. The mix for each of these four roles will vary depending on the requirement of the project. These roles are the marketing director, copywriter, artist and technical person (IT). If you are missing any of these skills on your team, then someone will have to take on double duty (this includes you). I highly recommend that you make sure that these skills are distinct from each other and outsource a skill completely if you need to.

You, as the CEO, are not included in this mix (yet). You are the visionary. You are the one who sets the objective. Your role in this mix will be made more clear when we start talking about Objectives, Strategies and Tactics in the next chapter.

Marketing Director

Next to the CEO, the marketing director has the most important role and must be in sync with the CEO's vision. The marketing director is responsible for making sure that the message for the website matches the business requirements and fits properly with the company's objectives. The marketing director should shield the CEO from elements that don't require his help, while encouraging involvement with any elements (such as brand image) that require his input.

At the end of the marketing initiative, it is the message of the company that must be conveyed. No marketing initiative can be effective without someone skilled organizing every aspect. Most good marketing companies (Web or otherwise) will take on this role for the small business and will work in concert with on-staff marketing directors for large companies.

The Five Dysfunctions of a Team: A Leadership Fable by Patrick Lencioni – The Five Dysfunctions of A Team is a great resource for team leaders and anyone who works in a team. Lencioni explores how to take a dysfunctional team and create success.

The marketing director is also responsible for design. When we talk about building the Web presence, we'll explore what this means.

Copywriter

My experience has been that the content for any marketing initiative is truly the hardest part. You'll find yourself in a bit of circular logic, because you'll want to see the artwork so you can write the content, but you can't complete the artwork until you have the content.

If you talk to most experienced Web developers, brochure creators, billboard designers and other commercial artists, you'll find one key similarity among all: content precedes design. Your content is the most important part. It needs to stand alone without the trappings of beautiful artwork.

Talented copywriters understand that your message is important no matter the picture. We say that a picture is worth 1,000 words, but before a picture is ever created, there were 1,000 words used to describe it. It is your copywriter's job to write the words for the artist to create the picture.

Artist

Artwork means nothing without a message behind it. Any good presentation requires content that is meaningful and a visual representation to support the message. An experienced graphic designer will expect an equally qualified content writer to produce the message so that the artwork has meaning.

The challenge most CEOs and marketing directors have with the graphical side of Web marketing is the misconception that the designer should make all of the decisions on how the website will look. What they fail to understand is that, in the absence of a clear, strategic objective and well-thought-out content, the artist is required to make too many assumptions as to the intent of the marketing initiative. A talented artist needs ambiguity removed and specific guidelines as to what is expected in order to create a visual presentation that supports the objectives of the company.

Technical

It is easy for someone with limited Web marketing experience to assume that the technical support should make the decisions for how the CEO's vision is translated to the Web. After all, the website is built on a server, using code that only technical people understand.

Today, website building tools are much easier than they used to be, and small businesses need limited technical support. More complicated Web applications and marketing initiatives require a more refined skill set.

As you define a strategic business direction, don't worry about what coding language or server technology is used. The IT person's role is to provide appropriate limitations

to streamline the business decision for the CEO. If budgets are a concern, then the IT person needs to make sure that the CEO knows what should be left out. He or she must be ready to provide reasonable alternatives to give the CEO the best possible options.

The hardest thing for any CEO is to delegate appropriate responsibilities. Usually, CEOs delegate the things they don't want to do. Rather, you need to limit your decisions to setting objectives. You'll want your marketing director to define the overarching strategy, while your copywriter, artist and technical person should define the appropriate tactics related to his or her function. Once you have defined the objective, each of the three key roles of copywriting, artistic and technical no longer report to you but to your "General," the marketing director.

HTML, CSS, XML, PHP, AJAX, JavaScript, JQuery, ASP.net, MySQL, SQL. – These are the various types of coding languages and databases used to build websites.

OBJECTIVES, STRATEGIES AND TACTICS

As a CEO, your role is to be the visionary of the company. Your vision should set the standard by which all of your employees operate. Leading your Web marketing strategies is the same. You are the visionary and should set the objectives for your company's marketing (on or offline) efforts.

Good to Great: Why Some Companies Make the Leap... and Others Don't by Jim Collins - Jim Collins explores the process of taking a good company to becoming a great company. As the CEO, you need to know what the difference between a good company and a great one, and how to get from point A to B.

Whenever you have an initiative in your business, there are three main parts: objectives, strategies and tactics. In order to accomplish any measure of success, it should always be handled in this order. Attempting to accomplish your initiatives in any other order would be akin to the concept of ready – fire – aim.

The easiest way to illustrate this concept is to compare it to home building. A few years ago, I decided to build my own home. I had never done it before, so it was a great challenge. I designed the home and had my stepfather draw up the plans. I was the general contractor, but I hired a friend to be a consultant to keep me on the right path. (There's a lesson there, too...don't assume you know everything).

Through that process, I realized how applicable the home building process is to so many other areas of our lives, especially business. While I will apply this process to online marketing, it applies to other facets of your business as well.

Consider building a home as a strategic process that has tactical components. There are three key roles in the home building process: homeowner, general contractor and subcontractors.

Homeowner

The homeowner is the visionary and has defined goals for what she wants in the home. She'll have certain things that are critically important in her mind and other things that are not as important. She'll have a primary objective, such as, "I want a 2,000 square foot, two-story home that has three bedrooms, two bathrooms, an office, a large pantry and a dog house for my husband. It all must fit within a budget of $83 per square foot." She'll also have secondary goals that are a bit more flexible, such as the location of the walls, how many square feet each room will have and what direction the home faces. Primary and secondary objectives fall into a concept called the commander's intent.

General Contractor

The general contractor is the strategist and makes sure that everything stays on track. His number one job is to ensure that the primary objective of the homeowner is met. In addition, he must adhere to the intent of the homeowner. The general contractor works with the various subcontractors to meet each of the objectives of the project. When the general contractor is building a speculation (spec) home, he will fulfill this role in addition to the role of the homeowner. Others who assist in the strategic process are those that help the general contractor define the plans for the home, such as the architect, truss designers and landscape designers, among others. In order for the homeowner to avoid costly decisions, the general contractor must educate the homeowner on the various steps in the process, as well as the high-level elements in the home building process.

Subcontractors

Subcontractors are the managers of the individual tasks, with their teams helping fulfill them. They have limited understanding of areas outside of their responsibility, at least by comparison to their own areas. The general contractor may not understand the details of the subcontractors' jobs; they are the specialists. They will make tactical decisions in their areas of stewardship.

If you have built a home, you may disagree that subcontractors are not strategic. First, you have to make sure that you don't confuse competence in tactical fulfillment with strategy.

Let's use the example of electrical, HVAC and plumbing. When I built my home, I, as the general contractor, scheduled all three of these subcontractors the same week for the

rough in. Each of them mentioned that they wanted to be first. At the beginning of the week, I didn't really understand why they wanted to be first. By the end of the week, I did.

When I planned my new home, it was very important to me where the electrical outlets were. I cared about the locations of each of the sinks, hose bibs and the ever-important toilets. I didn't really care too much where the vents, cold air returns or thermostats went.

My home plans indicated where all the sinks and toilets were to go, but the plumber walked me through to make sure he knew that the plans (strategy) correlated with reality. I was interested to note that the electrician used the home plans as the loosest of guidelines. We walked through every room in the house, marked on the wall where every single outlet was to go and marked the floor right below where a light fixture was to be placed. The electrician did some simple math to determine how many circuits would be needed for my home. The HVAC contractor, on the other hand, wanted to exactly understand my intent of a dual-zone cooling system, and we talked about vent and thermostat position to come up with the right approach to accomplish my goals.

For the most part, walking through my home and putting some marks on the walls and floors was the extent of our planning. From there, it was a race for each of the three subcontractors to use the ideal locations in the walls for pipes, conduits and tubes. The only thing they were concerned about was the shortest distance from point a to point b.

If my home had been a commercial building, then each of the subcontractors would have had a detailed plan of where every element would be.

Primary Objective – Your main focus. There should always be only one primary objective, such as creating a high quality product for your consumers, increasing your presence on the Web or becoming a resource within your field. Note – just because you only should have one Primary Objective does not mean to not work towards other objectives. This is your main focus, not your only focus.

What is tactical thinking?

Picture this: it's Saturday morning and you have a list of ten things that need to get done. Do you sit down and make a plan of how you are going to do it? When I say a plan, I mean more than, "Between 8:00 a.m. and 10:00 a.m., I'll work on the lawn, and then I'll start building my hamster run."

Generally speaking, you create a list of tasks and work on them in the order that you like. If you are smart about it, you tackle the easy tasks first so that you can feel a sense of accomplishment.

When I talk about tactical thinking, I mean that we think of the individual things that we have to do, rather than looking at the big picture and how the various elements fit together. It is easier to think tactically. We don't have to worry about planning or, more importantly, not accomplishing a plan.

One of the biggest challenges for any marketer (on or offline) is to stop thinking tactically. All too often, marketing decisions are based on the advice given by the same person that sells advertising. If a business owner has a strong rapport with the radio salesperson, he'll turn to that same salesperson for advice about marketing.

Now, let me be clear: the radio, TV or print rep may, in fact, have good advice. That person may be very intelligent. But, let's not fool ourselves—that person is paid to sell advertising.

If the advertising rep gives you advice about your strategic marketing direction, it is like the idea that when your only tool is a hammer, then every problem is a nail.

Too often, we look at the items that we have to sell and consider them as the "solution." Then, it's just a matter of finding the right problem to solve. Strategic thinking involves looking at the problems we have and then finding the solution to fit that problem. It means looking at business objectives with open eyes and recognizing that we may not have all the answers just yet.

Each subcontractor for my home simply came in, fulfilled the measure of their tactical requirement and then went home. They did a great job, but there was no real strategy. They were focused on making sure that the strategic plan (blueprint) was implemented properly.

As the CEO, you are the homeowner. You need to understand enough to set the vision properly. You'll need the help of your strategist to do it right. That strategist (the general contractor) could be someone on staff, such as a marketing director, or it could be a person or company that you hire to complete the project for you. The subcontractors for your Web project are the graphic designers, programmers, content writers and technical support staff.

The hardest part about marketing, if you are like most CEOs, is to understand where the strategy stops and the tactics begin. It can be a challenge to understand whose role is most important. Your job is to make sure that the objective and intent are properly defined, while allowing each person to fulfill his or her purpose.

LOST IN THE CORN FIELD

When you consider your Web presence, you may be thinking that if you build it, your clients will come. All too often I hear from clients, "I spent $10,000 on my website, and it is really pretty. Why are people not coming to my site?"

There are many answers as to why this might be, but the easiest way to answer this is to understand that there is no such thing as a field of dreams. If you build it, they may not come.

Your website is no different. Just because you have a pretty site, it doesn't mean people will come. And, sometimes more importantly, just because you have a pretty site, it doesn't mean that first-time visitors will choose to come back.

We can look back to the example of Vin Fiz. Tens of thousands of people knew about the "Ideal Grape Drink," but the product never took off. Just because it was there—or, moreover, just because people knew it was there—wasn't enough reason to cause people to buy the product. Never assume that, just because you do something that you think is noteworthy, everyone else will agree.

Consider this: you'll have a certain number of people who will be your customers no matter what you do. Generally speaking, that number is lower than your real break-even point. They'll come to you no matter how bad your service is, how rude you are or how much your brand sucks. Most businesses that fail simply have costs that outweigh the number of people that "get it." I have seen too many bad sales and business people succeed to think otherwise.

The real key to business is capturing a meaningful audience. And, with more

> Where did we come from? You wouldn't believe how many guys wanted to play here. We had to beat 'em off with a stick.
> – Shoeless Joe Jackson, Field of Dreams

than 75 percent of North America's population online, there is a pretty good chance that, if you're not online with a meaningful presence, you won't capture the audience that can really make your business grow. But, remember, just because you are online, there is no guarantee they will come, but when they do, you better be ready to capture their attention.

I don't want you to be discouraged. Just because people may not come to your website, doesn't mean that you should give up now. Understanding this is what is going to help you build your Web presence in a way that will be meaningful for your clients.

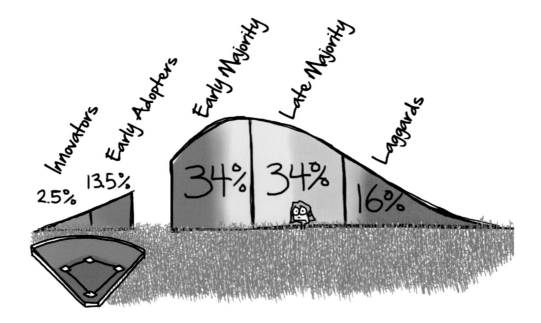

In Geoffrey Moore's *Crossing the Chasm*, he discusses the chasm between the early adopters and mass-market appeal. When you think that just because you build it people will naturally come you are making an assumption that people are actively looking for you. You might get a few people to see your *Field of Dreams* but be careful. Most people will simply be lost in the corn.

Every Web presence that has attracted the desired traffic has utilized the key principles of great online marketing. Some have the ability to draw people seemingly automatically (virally) because the website is so compelling (think Amazon, Facebook and Apple), but even they didn't get there just because they existed. They worked hard to develop an online brand that was meaningful to their audience.

> *Crossing the Chasm* by Geoffrey Moore – Crossing the Chasm focuses on marketing high-tech products. It has implications in the marketing of all new ideas, including your Web presence.

THE FIRST 10 SECONDS

Being online is your opportunity to tell people how you are different. It is your opportunity to be unique. It is your chance to not be generic.

I am constantly amazed at how many business leaders I speak to are so excited about their unique selling proposition. "We are so different from any of our competitors," they say.

As I ask them to tell me more about how they are different, they successfully tell me all the things they do that are exactly like their competitors. Invariably, I find that the only difference is that they have a different name for what they do. This only means that they have to teach their customers a new term, which is usually a mash up of two words that don't mean anything or a completely made up word that has mystical properties. If the real difference is that you call your ham sandwich a Hamtween Bread, you aren't going to be very impressive.

It is critically important, as you look at your Web presence, that you understand it is a great amplifier of who you are. And, the first goal is to realize where you are different so that you can amplify that difference online. Take Apple computers, for example. They are different because of a great product, spectacular messaging and a unique culture, but they still only sell computers. Or, consider Zappos, a company that is spectacular because of a clean Web presence, a unique go to marketing strategy and, again, a unique culture. They still only sell shoes. The key here is that these two brands use their websites to extend their skillful marketing, copy and design, rather than recreate a new, unrelated (but pretty) Web presence. If you can't do this in 10 seconds or less, your differences really don't matter.

This book does not (intentionally) talk about branding. That is an entire discussion all unto itself. Yet, understanding who you are is a critically important step to understanding how to present yourself online.

A picture is worth a thousand words. An interface is worth a thousand pictures
– Ben Shneiderman

KEEPIN' IT REAL

Years ago, as a sales manager, I was asked to develop a brochure for my company. Aside from the fact that a sales manager should never be assigned to the task of creating an effective marketing piece, there were a number of key problems with the development of this brochure. The process I went through is critical to understanding the problems with trying to "fake" your way through the marketing process.

Since I was asked to create this brochure, I went through a number of iterations of what I wanted it to say, but I just couldn't come up with anything that made sense. I had a background in graphic design, so this should have been easy. Shoot, I had just come from a job as the Color Systems Specialist for the Western United States for Canon USA...I knew how to do this. But, alas, I couldn't get it done for the life of me.

On the fourth or fifth try, I took it to the president, and he finally gave me the content that he wanted in the document. My response was simple, "But we don't do any of that."

He told me that it didn't matter. "We just need to say what we want people to think about us, and then we can figure out how to pull it off later," he said.

I tried a few more times to get something compelling out, but it ended up being hollow. It just didn't make sense to be inauthentic...it would come back and bite us in the posterior.

After a few more tries, the project was finally taken off my hands (thankfully). The president wrote the content he wanted. He hired an outside graphic designer who made it "pretty" (it wasn't really). Then, he printed 1,000 full color fliers that were never used by anyone.

Not long after this, the brochure was converted to an ineffective website that looked just as "pretty" as the brochure (and was used about as much).

Oatmeal vs. Bacon by Justin Foster - Oatmeal vs. Bacon gives insight into why some brands dominate and others don't. Is your company Oatmeal or is it Bacon?

In thinking about the experience, I realized that there are three key areas that need to be addressed when thinking about marketing. Get these three areas wrong and your message won't hold water—on or offline.

These three areas of marketing are listed in order of importance.

Brand

Contrary to popular belief, brand is not your logo. Your logo is simply a mark that represents your brand. If a logo is all a brand is, then there is even less excuse to have a bad brand. Rather, your brand is a definition of who you are. It is your culture. It is the way you interact internally as well as externally. Even bad brands have a brand. The personal equivalent to brand is your character.

Brand Identity

Brand identity is the way you look, and this is really where your logo fits. It is the colors you choose and the way you present your messages. It is not your message, but how it looks when presented. The personal equivalent to brand identity is how you dress and groom yourself.

Content

Content is what you say. It is how you verbally and nonverbally communicate your brand. Don't confuse content with written content only; it also includes pictures and videos. It is the words and imagery you use to communicate your message. The personal equivalent to content is the words that you speak and your nonverbal gestures and expressions.

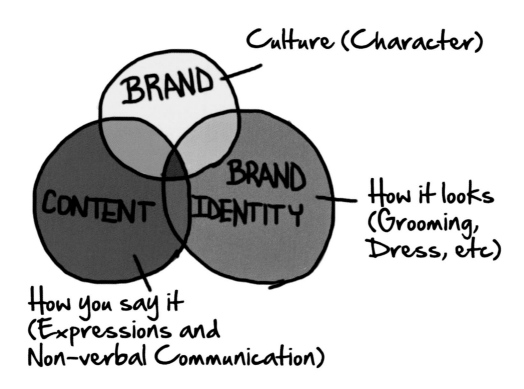

When creating our company brochure, we certainly had a brand. We knew who we were. We even had a brand identity. We had a logo and colors we used. What we didn't have, however, was content that matched who we were. Therefore, it failed.

If you fail in creating a brochure, your failure is probably small. You may be out a few dollars (unless you are stupid enough to mail it to a large audience). A website, on the other hand, is of more importance. Because the World Wide Web is a great magnifier, you run the risk of your website being a large failure. It likely costs more to create than a brochure and has the potential of being seen by many more people.

All three parts—brand, brand identity and content—need to work in concert in order to effectively communicate who you are. If you have a great brand but your website sucks, it's like wearing sweats to a business meeting. If you aren't Mark Zuckerberg, then this probably isn't a good idea. Likewise, if you try to hide who you are in the minutia of content, you will lose every single time. You have to be authentic.

BRINGING IT ALL TOGETHER

At this point, you might be thinking, "So what? How do I make all of this work?"

Let's look back to our story of the Vin Fiz Flyer to tie it together. Every good strategy starts with an objective, and Cal's objective was to reach the West Coast in 30 days. Strategically, he needed to provide for the logistics of the task. So, he enlisted the support of Armour and Company to provide the funding, support train and crew to rebuild the plane as he crashed. Part of the strategy was to follow the railroad the entire way so that the support train would be close as he crashed his way across the United States.

Cal's tactics changed on a day-to-day basis. He didn't know, from the beginning, exactly what problems he would face. If he was rigid in the tactics he chose, he might never have made it across the country. Most people who are too rigid in tactical execution of a well-thought-out strategic plan end up throwing up their arms in defeat. Luckily, Cal wasn't one of those people.

I have the opportunity to talk with business owners on a regular basis. Sometimes, I'll hear comments that the economy is poor; other times, I'll hear that things couldn't be better. Business is good for those who learn to roll with the times and how to adapt and change with the realities of the current marketing conditions.

As Helmuth von Moltke the Elder said, "No plan of operations extends with certainty beyond the first encounter with the enemy's main strength." He is also often quoted as saying, "No plan survives contact with the enemy." While we never want to consider our customers the enemy, this quote's application to marketing is significant. A well-laid plan can allow us to be far more successful in our go-to-market strategy, but the willingness to be flexible in that plan can mean the difference between success and failure.

> No plan of operations extends with certainty beyond the first encounter with the enemy's main strength." And "No plan survives contact with the enemy.
> – Helmuth von Moltke The Elder

Your tactics, by necessity, will change as you begin to execute your strategy. Your job, as CEO, is to define the strategy and let your team determine the right tactics to fulfill their part of the plan.

FOUNDATIONAL WEB MARKETING

In order to fully understand how to create a good Web strategy, you need a general understanding of the elements of online marketing. If you don't know what is possible, you won't know what to consider.

There are two main areas to online marketing: Web presence and Web marketing. The next two main sections of this book will dive deeper into each of these areas.

To understand this concept and further explore tactical versus strategic marketing, I'd like to introduce a concept that I call the Foundational Approach to Web Marketing. In the following pages, I'll build on this concept one layer at a time. To fully appreciate how this works, we actually need to approach the subject backwards, starting with the end and then showing the beginning (sort of like Star Wars).

More and more, I see advertising that talks about the latest and greatest thing you can do in getting the word out about your business. Depending on whom you talk to, the method will have varying levels of predicted success. These tactics must change from business to business, market to market and objective to objective. The measured level of success is usually a direct correlation to how the person you are talking to is being compensated. In other words, when talking to your radio rep, radio is this shiz. When talking to your yellow pages rep, yellow pages are the cat's meow. You get the idea.

The problem is that you find yourself taking advice from the same person that is selling to you. This person will give you stats that will prove their point. Remember, stats never lie, but liars use stats.

I always love the billboard that says, "See, you just proved that advertising works." No, all it proved was that I saw it, not that it accomplished anything.

I tend to think that the most effective advertising is that which really sells itself...but it doesn't really exist, so you have to know how to stop thinking tactically (radio vs. billboard vs. Google vs. email) and start thinking strategically (how all the methods tie together). If advertising sold itself, then there would be no need for advertising sales reps.

For a successful Web marketing (or general marketing) plan to be effective, this top-down, strategic thinking must be at the core of the plan—headed up by a knowledge-able CEO, like yourself, who is ready to make a good business decision. In the next sections, I will help you with the knowledge part by examining the two mains aspects of online marketing.

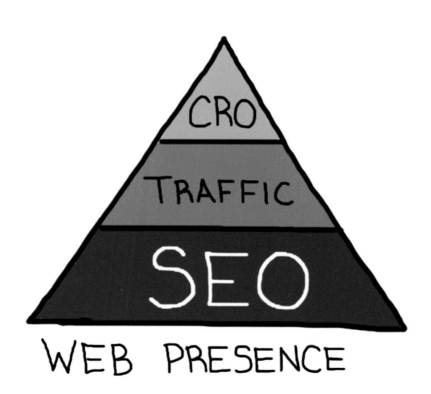

FOUNDATIONAL WEB MARKETING,

METHODOLOGY

 The foundation of your Web marketing efforts is your Web presence. This Web presence can be your Facebook page or a simple landing page. Most often, this Web presence is your website. It provides the location for your site visitors to find you online.

 Just because you have a Web presence, there is no guarantee that you'll be found in the search engines like Google, Yahoo! or Bing. For that, we need search engine optimization or SEO. SEO helps your Web presence appear higher in the search engines.

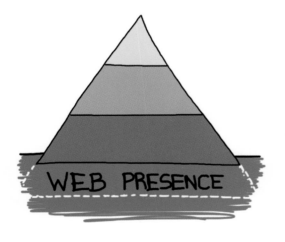

CONTINUED

Just because you are ranked in the search engines, there is no guarantee that people will find you. Traffic generation allows to drive visitors to your Web presence. SEO can provide traffic but other tactics may include social media marketing, pay-per-click advertising and email marketing.

Just because you have traffic to your Web presence, there is no guarantee that people will buy from you, give you a lead or do what you want. Conversion rate optimization (CRO) allows your site to be optimized to get people to do more of what you want more often.

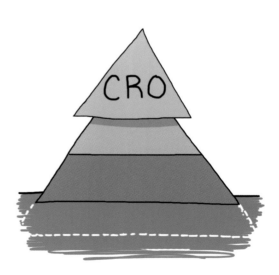

Web Presence

A DREAM

Until I was about 13 years old, my family lived about 30 miles from Disneyland, which gave me the opportunity to go often. I remember the introduction of the all-day pass—rides were no longer ticketed, and I was finally able to ride any ride with the price of admission.

As a child, I compared every amusement park I went to with Disneyland. It didn't matter if it was an expensive park, such as Knott's Berry Farm or Six Flags Magic Mountain, or if it was a less expensive park like the Los Angeles County Fair. Nothing could hold a candle to the magic that Disneyland held.

This magic is no accident. As Walt Disney sat at an amusement park watching his young daughters play, he noticed how filthy and in disrepair the place was. I am sure you can relive his experience by going to most any carnival or fair today an hour after it opens.

He thought there must be a better way. In fact, he said,

What this country really needs is an amusement park that families can take their children to. They've gotten so honky tonk with a lot of questionable characters running around, and they're not too safe. They're not well kept. I want to have a place that's as clean as anything could ever be, and all the people in it [his park] are first-class citizens, and treated like guests.

Walt spent several years thinking about what he wanted and planning his vision. He knew that he wanted an experience for his guests that they would never forget. His first idea was to create "Mickey Mouse Park" with a themed Main Street, Western village, land of tomorrow and more. These initial ideas later developed into Disneyland.

ALL YOUR DREAMS CAN COME TRUE IF YOU HAVE THE COURAGE TO PURSUE THEM.
– WALT DISNEY

On July 17th, 1955, Disneyland opened to thousands of people who streamed through the front gate. There were only 11,000 invited to the opening day but, because the tickets were so easily reproduced, attendance soared to over 28,000. In addition to these unprecedented numbers, an estimated 90,000 people viewed the opening on ABC. Walt stood at the window of the apartment he'd built for himself above the fire station on Main Street (a place that has fond memories for me personally) and watched as people came into the park for the first time. Just like people today, I'll bet their eyes widened with wonder as they stepped foot in the new park.

A Mouseketeer named Sharon Baird stood with him that day. Of the experience, she said,

I was standing next to him at the window, watching the guests come through the gates. When I looked up at him, he had his hands behind his back, a grin from ear to ear, and I could see a lump in his throat and a tear streaming down his cheek. He had realized his dream.

Shortly after, Walt envisioned something bigger, and Walt Disney World soon followed with the Magic Kingdom and Epcot (Experimental Prototype Community of Tomorrow) and the other parks in Orlando, Florida.

Today, millions of people visit the various Disney parks and shops of Downtown Disney, not to mention the stores in cities around the world, radio, television and the movies. Throughout it all, one thing remains constant: Walt Disney's original vision of a family friendly location where children can enjoy the magic of childhood endures.

Not long ago, a person that I follow on Twitter asked about a good place to buy a trampoline. Immediately, I responded with a link to the Google Places page of the company I bought mine from (this company didn't have a website), saying that there was no better place to buy a trampoline. Not long after, another person replied to my recommendation and agreed. You can't pay for that type of advertising—it is immediately relevant and applicable.

YOUR BRAND IS EVERYWHERE

You should consider your Web presence as a location where your customers engage with you. You won't have only one location. Consider your Web presence any location on the Web where your customers will engage with you. Primarily, we think about your Web presence as your website. Before we get too deep in talking specifically about your website, let's examine the essence of Disney and how the company aptly applies its brand and vision to everything it touches.

Disney's "presence" is not limited to one location or meaning. Rather, it depends on context, conversation and many other factors. On the West Coast of the United States, a Disney vacation is probably to Disneyland. On the East Coast, the same vacation is probably to Walt Disney World. Disney understands this and uses regionally based advertising to direct people to the location that they are most likely to travel to.

Content Rules by Ann Handley – Discover the best ways your business can communicate with its customers over the web. This book explores blogs, YouTube, Facebook, Twitter and many more ways you can reach out to your customer base.

In addition to your personal mental picture of the Disney presence, the company is continually working to add more. In recent years, they have been pushing to expand their cruise line. In doing so, they do it right by adhering to Walt Disney's original vision. I've been on a Disney cruise with my wife, and it holds true to his ideal of a family friendly environment.

The most contiguous message of the Disney brand, across all Disney properties, is the vision of a location where families can take children. When looking at Disney branded movies or even adult-oriented attractions, there is the core philosophy of family values infused in every aspect of the experience.

Using Disney as a model, there are a few things you need to understand about your Web presence.

Not One Location

Your Web presence is not limited to one location. Your main Web presence is your website, which is where your primary audience engages directly with you. This is also where they will go to get information about you and your company. For a business, this is likely the location where most of your client interaction will take place, especially if you are selling products directly online.

However, your Web presence extends to other areas as well, including social media locations like Twitter, Facebook, YouTube and LinkedIn. In fact, when thinking about your location being social media, you'll find it will encompass audiences from all demographic groups. In addition, your Web presence extends to places that you can't control, such as community driven pages like Yelp, Google and Foursquare. Over the years, the names of these venues may change, but the concept of user driven feed-back will be true for many years to come.

You Can't Hide

No matter how hard you try to avoid it, you will be judged according to your Web presence (or lack thereof). People will judge you by how accessible you are online. Simply ignoring the need for a Web presence will not make the problem go away; if anything, it will only exacerbate it.

Content Is King

Content is what matters most. This means all types of content, not just words. Whether it is static or hybrid content, it is very important to how you are perceived by visitors to your website. In fact, this is one key reason why social media increases in popularity on a regular basis—it provides immediately relevant information. Your website should be where your most important content is located and, from there, you should make sure that it is pushed to all your content distribution channels .

MINIMUM VIABLE PRODUCT

What if Walt Disney had waited until everything was complete before opening Disneyland Park? What if he had decided to wait for any new ideas that might come, stalling the opening of the park another five to ten years? What if he'd said, "Let's wait until Splash Mountain or the Indiana Jones ride are complete to open."

Surely Walt made certain that everything looked nice and was well thought out, but the park was not complete when it opened. It was complete enough to open, but it still had things that needed to be built and added. If he had waited until it was complete, the park never would have opened as there are new things being built each day.

> When you work in a state of constant preparation, you never get to start selling.
> – Corey Smith

If we compare your website to Disneyland (my bet is that your website isn't as fun, but work with me here), then we can consider each feature of your site as a particular ride, show or attraction.

THIS ROAD TO BE EXTENDED IN THE FUTURE.

> Your minimum viable product needs to be the minimum required to produce a fully functioning product but not more. Keep it simple.

When Disneyland first opened, there were attractions such as "Jungle Cruise," "Mr. Toad's Wild Ride" and "Tomorrowland," but "It's a Small World" didn't open for another year. Likewise, your website should launch when the core requirements are complete. Additional features can be added later as they are completed. Remember, think back to your primary objective, which is to create a Web presence that engages your main audience and serves as the first interaction with a new or existing customer.

This concept is called the minimum viable product. There is no hard and fast rule that can tell you what the minimum viable product is, because it will be different for every company and situation. It might be that you have users who are accustomed to a certain experience and, at minimum, that experience has to be maintained. If you have an eCommerce site, you will expect that your website includes a shopping cart and can accept credit cards. However, if you don't have a website, then maybe your minimum viable product is a splash page that has your phone number and a simple contact form.

I have seen various companies' marketing efforts put on hold because they try to make their first site far exceed the minimum viable product. When you work in a state of constant preparation, you never get to start selling.

OBJECTIVES FIRST

When you are working to define your minimum viable product, you must first define your primary objective. Notice that "objective" is singular and not plural. You only need one primary objective.

> What you do is proof of what you believe.
> – Simon Sinek

Walt's primary objective was a safe place that families could take their children. He wasn't focused on the coolest rides, best attractions or most shops. There is no doubt that Disneyland is very commercial. But, while the rides are incredible, the shows are top notch and there are plenty of ways for you to spend your money, that was not the primary objective of Walt's dream.

When you define your primary objective, everything else will start to come together. Let me rephrase that (because I am too lazy to hit the back space on my keyboard), when you define, focus on and adhere to elements that support your primary objective, everything else will start to come together. It really is the adhering to your primary objective that allows you to accomplish your goals.

Don't get me wrong—you should have plenty of other objectives. I am sure that Walt wanted to be profitable. In fact, shortly after opening Disneyland Park, he commented, "We're gonna kick ourselves for not buying everything within a radius of ten miles around here." He recognized that his primary objective would only be met by achieving commercial success and that there were certain things that would allow him to do so. He didn't know for sure because he had to test it first, but he had a pretty good idea.

You will have ideas for your Web presence. You will have certain things that you think are important. In the end, it really doesn't matter what you think. It matters what your customers do with what you think.

What's your primary objective?

When I look at the successes and failures in business, I think I have found a consistency between them.

The successful businesses remember their primary objective and the businesses that fail forget what they are working for.

Let's put a practical example with this concept.

I am not sure that anyone would disagree that Harley-Davidson is a pretty incredible brand. In fact, Justin Foster (Author, *Oatmeal v. Bacon*) calls Harley-Davidson a bacon brand. At one point, like many brands, Harley lost it's way. It found its way back, almost by the skin of it's teeth and has emerged more powerful than ever.

Among all this, one of the key reasons it is a successful brand is because they are careful to remember their primary objective... their primary mission. Harley's mission is:

"We ride with our customers and apply this deep connection in every market we serve to create superior value for all our stakeholders."

It is through this commitment to one, single, defining objective that make businesses successful. When businesses forget who they are and try to split their focus, they find themselves in a position of losing power and heading for a great fall.

Perhaps this is the problem with the yahoos in Washington (no offense meant to Yahoo!). There is not one, single, defining objective for anyone in Washington right now... perhaps not since Ronald Reagan has there been any unifying focus.

Congress is focused on getting re-elected and their own pet projects.

[Insert Politician's Name] is focused on jobs -- no healthcare -- no blaming [Insert Other Politician's Name] -- no jobs -- no fundraising -- no "the war" -- no jobs -- no social problems -- I think you get the idea.

Political ideals aside, I defy you to point to any one objective that Washington is focused on. I mean really focused on. I'm talking about a prime directive that everyone looks to when a new program or a new idea is proposed and asks, "How does this thing help us to meet our primary objective? "

I don't care if you are running a small business or a large business. I don't care if you are creating a marketing plan or setting a home budget. I don't care if you are tasked with running a country. If you don't know what your primary objective is, you are going to flounder. If you don't get to the point that you can finally figure it out... well, then you will fail. And when you fail, you will fail spectacularly.

STRATEGIC BLUEPRINT

After you have defined your primary objective (and probably understand a few of your other objectives), then you are ready to start planning your website. It's time to begin thinking about how your site is going to be built.

Now, you might be asking, "We were talking before about Web presence, and now we are at the website. How can I keep these concepts straight?"

Good question, thanks for asking.

Your objectives will apply to whatever you consider your Web presence. If your Web presence is Facebook or LinkedIn, then it will apply there. However, the most important Web presence you have is your website; it is the foundation of your Web marketing efforts. Because of this, I tend to use Web presence and website inter-

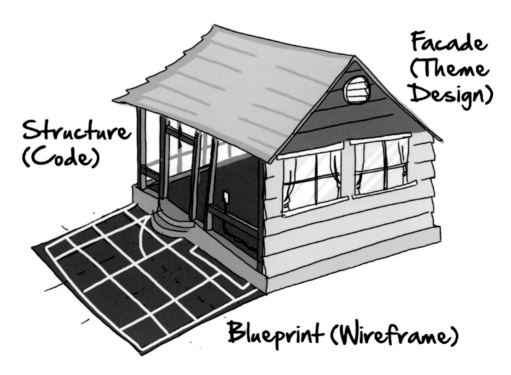

Structure (Code)

Facade (Theme Design)

Blueprint (Wireframe)

changeably. We'll talk about building a strategic plan for your marketing in the last section of this book.

Your strategic plan is going to have three main components. Sure, you'll probably need help on this, but remember that your job, as the visionary, is not to build the site or even directly manage the site (unless you choose to). Rather, you need to understand what it takes to build the site so that you can set realistic objectives that your team can fulfill.

Content Outline / Sitemap

Your content is the most important part of your site. It is the information that will be conveyed. This includes text, images and video.

Wireframe (User Interface / Layout)

A wireframe is the layout of a site. This has nothing to do with your brand. It is how people will find their way around your site, void of any branding elements such as logos and colors.

Graphics (Decoration)

Graphic design is where the artist gets his or her piece of the pie. While this aspect is important, remember that the content defines what should be included, the wireframe defines where it should be included and the graphics define how it should be included.

Each of these three elements must have decisions made to create the appropriate strategy. Because of the importance of these elements, we will explore each in detail in the coming pages.

Web Design for ROI by Lance Loveday – Proper website design doesn't just mean making your website look good. There is much more to creating a successful website, such as proper SEO. This book will help you learn to maximize returns from your website.

6 KEY ELEMENTS

As you think about the website that you will develop, there are some key considerations. You want to make sure that you design it right; if you don't, you might just be wasting your time and money.

But, what are the key things that you should consider? These elements are in no particular order.

Core Site Content

Search engines love content, and they need it to find your website. The more content you have, the more opportunity your site has to be indexed by Google, Yahoo and Bing. If you don't have compelling core site content that includes heavily searched key words, search engines won't find you... and neither will potential customers.

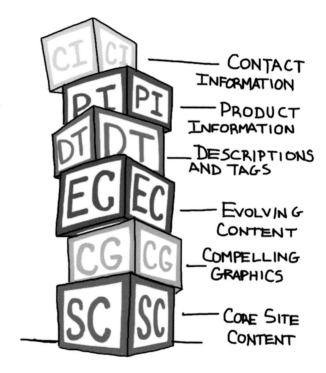

- CONTACT INFORMATION
- PRODUCT INFORMATION
- DESCRIPTIONS AND TAGS
- EVOLVING CONTENT
- COMPELLING GRAPHICS
- CORE SITE CONTENT

Compelling Graphics

While website content is key for search engines, graphics are key for the user experience. There is a fine line to walk here—too many images make it harder for the search engines to find a site, while too few may make a site kind of boring.

WEB PRESENCE

Evolving Content

Even if the search engines find you, it doesn't mean people will stay on your site. If your website's content is not relevant, a user may quickly move on. And, the older your content gets, the less relevant it is. The easiest way to have new content is to post news and opinion (blog) articles on your site. It is not hard to write a blog post; it just takes a few minutes.

Descriptions and Tags

Each page on your website should have unique descriptions and tags. Most websites I visit have the same descriptions and tags on every page (if they have them at all). These should be accurate but not overdone. These unique descriptions and tags are never seen by website visitors but are read by search engines. For this to be effective, the content writer needs to make sure tags are written, and the site programmer needs to code them properly.

Product Information

There is nothing worse than an interested customer having to leave your website to learn more about your product. All of your product information should be on your website, and it should be easy for customers to find the information they are looking for. If they can't find it, then you need to rethink your content.

Contact Information

When customers can't find contact information on a company's website, it can be frustrating. Even though so much is done online nowadays, people still use the phone. They still want to pick up the phone and hear a live voice; they still want to know your

---

Meta Keywords – The keywords that describe the content on a specific page. These help search engines distinguish important content on a page and ties into search rankings.

Meta Description – A written description of your pages content. This is a tool that helps search engines categorize your content and ties into search rankings.

address to see if you are near them or not. Your contact information should be prominent and easily accessible.

Certainly, these are very broad elements that should be included in your website. Each scenario is going to be different, and I can only hope to give you the guidelines of what the end result should look like. It will take strategic planning to make sure the right elements are included in your Web presence.

THE SYSTEM

A number of years ago, before I owned a web company, I was tasked with building my first commercial website for the company I worked for. I found it to be a very challenging process, and we ended up going live with a website that was woefully incomplete. There were holes in several (most) of the pages. After the website was live, a coworker and I scrambled to get things done. You see, while we thought we had certain things done, we kept finding page after page of "content goes here".

I've often thought back to that experience and wondered what went wrong. In doing so, I realized that one of the key problems was that we didn't follow a defined process; because we didn't have a good strategy, we didn't know what was left to accomplish. I now realize that building a website is very much like building a house.

In the first section of the book, I told the story of building my home for the first time. In doing so, I analyzed how the homeowner, general contractor and subcontractors were similar to those involved in a marketing strategy. I also learned through the process of building my home that there are four primary steps that correlate directly to building

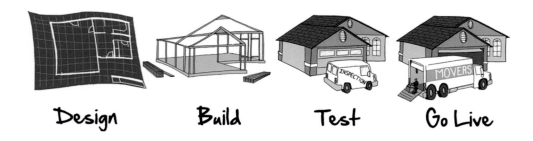

Design   Build   Test   Go Live

a website. I have built hundreds of websites over the last few years and have found that every time I deviate from this process, things go downhill fast. If you look at it from a homebuilder's perspective, it will be easier to understand why.

> We can't solve problems by using the same kind of thinking we used when we created them.
> – Albert Einstein

Design

Design always comes first. Could you imagine building a home without having a design—a blueprint—first? In reality, a blueprint is the strategy of how to build the home. Your website is no different, and you need a plan to be able to build the website right. This is where you set the direction for the content, layout and graphics of your site. You may not finalize the colors or images, but the direction should be set.

In the blueprint of a house, where the walls go and how everything is put together is extremely important. Once the walls go up, it is very expensive to go back and move them. Similarly, the design phase is where structural decisions are made, saving you time and money in the end.

In furthering this comparison, think of a house as the website and furniture and decorations as the content. Most people don't consider furniture and decorations when designing a home, or at least they don't realize they do. It's a given that there will be beds in the bedrooms and a couch and TV in the family room. The blueprints allow for this...most of the time. I've lived in a few different homes that lacked storage closets, had awkward layouts to accommodate couches and TVs and didn't leave adequate space for dining room tables. When you don't take into consideration the content (furniture) when designing your website (house), things don't fit. The more you know about what will go into the website before you start building it, the better everything will fit and the easier it will be to get things done. Just like in Star Wars, you have to work backwards.

Televisions are all the same, or are they?

When I added high definition to my satellite TV, my eyes were opened to a new way of watching TV. I already had a quality, high definition television but I hadn't watched a football game or live news in high definition. I had no idea what I was missing. I had no idea that there was so much to be seen.

In my home, I also have some older TVs that are not high definition capable. They produce a great picture, for the type of TV they are. However, they do not have the ability to show all the colors and details that my high definition TV can offer.

Even my high definition TV can't show the breadth of what is available on the market such as newer, more capable TVs including 3D TV.

Your website is no different. There are many browser types out there. Internet Explorer, Chrome and Firefox are the three most popular browsers for viewing websites. However, they each have different capabilities and will render, or display, your website differently. It doesn't make them wrong, it just is what it is.

Build

This is what I call the "fingers-on-keyboards" phase; it's where programmers start putting it together. Since the beginning of our company, we have called this the assembly phase; this is where the programming, configuration of back-end elements (which no business person should ever have to worry about) and addition of the content to the website take place. It also includes applying all of the color elements, adding the content to pages and making the last minute decisions for graphics.

It looks fine in Firefox, so it should work perfectly in Internet Explorer and Google Chrome.

BS Meter - 5/5

Generally speaking, this should not take longer than the design phase. My experience has been that the actual building of a website takes a small fraction of the design time. At this point, no more decisions usually need to be made and fingers are free to plug away at the keyboard. There are two key exceptions to this rule:

1. The design phase wasn't completed properly. For example, this can happen if the content or graphics aren't complete or decisions are still being made about the structure.

2. There are significant technical requirements, such as a custom Web application that needs to be built. Time can be saved at this stage if planning has been done properly in the design phase.

During the build phase, it's understandable that not all the design decisions will have been made. There will always be elements that weren't considered because you may not have understood what to consider. However, there should be few decisions. If you find that you are making too many decisions as you build your website, then you probably didn't spend enough time during the design phase.

Testing

If you decide to hire someone else to build your house, the testing phase starts at the final walkthrough. The first part is simply you walking through the house with the builder and putting little marks on the walls (usually with blue painter's tape) so they can touch up certain elements.

Each website should have a testing period. The more complicated the website, the longer the testing phase should be. For relatively small websites, say 5 to 10 pages, it can be as short as an hour, with a few people looking at it. If it is a website with complicated components, such as eCommerce, photo galleries or social interaction, then the testing phase should be much longer and involve many people to put the it through its paces.

If you decide that you are going to build the website in-house with your own employees, then the testing phase may require you to get outside help to properly test the site. When you get close to the project during the design and build phase, it's hard to notice the little errors. Others will see errors that you've been staring at for weeks, and they'll wonder how you could possibly have missed them.

Go Live

Going live with your website is akin to moving in to your home and starting to live there. However, it's not necessarily as momentous an occasion as you might have hoped, and the neighbors won't know you're there unless you tell them (that's what the third section of the book is for). Similarly, launching your site does not magically let everyone know that it is up and running; going live is simply a flip of a virtual switch.

I mentioned earlier that the testing phase starts with a final walkthrough. The testing phase can continue (and usually does) after the website has gone live. You'll find that,

no matter how many eyes look at your website, there will always be a problem that was missed. Someone will have forgotten to put a picture in the right spot, add a link or dot an i .

The moral of this is that going live is not an end to your website project. It is a start to your marketing efforts. With that in mind, your goal is to get your site live as soon as you can. Think back to the minimum viable product, and remember that you can add more content to your website as easily as you can bring more furniture into your house.

These steps in the process often get a little muddied, and it takes discipline to follow the process. Just remember: the better you adhere to this process, the more likely you are to have a streamlined project that ends with a website you can be proud of.

CONTENT TRUMPS DESIGN

Too often I hear CEOs talk about how pretty they want their website to be. They go on about how they want a big button for chat or to showcase all of their products on their homepage (with pictures of baby narwhals because narwhals are magical).

I then ask the ever-fateful question: "Okay, what do you want your website to say?"

Blank stares.

Begin with Why by SImon Sinek – Simon Sinek explores why some individuals and organizations are more innovative, influential, and profitable than others. There are many questions to ask in business, but you must start with "why."

It doesn't matter how pretty your website is if you don't have a message that matters. It doesn't matter how many features you have if your content sucks.

In my opinion, the content is actually the hardest part of any Web project, because it is the heart of the strategy for the website. You can't have a

> Blogs – Opinion pieces written by various people in your company
>
> Articles – Documents that illustrate a point. In the tech industry these are called whitepapers.
>
> News Stories – AKA Press Releases - Good opportunity to showcase your clients work and gain placement from news outlets.

website without words and pictures. If the picture doesn't have a story to tell, then the 1,000 words it uses aren't worth a whole lot.

As mentioned before, content is king. Let's review exactly what content is before we go too far. While most people assume that content is limited to words, it is only one part of a site's content.

Let's look at a few of the different types of content.

Images

Images aren't just photos; they are also graphs, charts, diagrams, arrows and other visual items that attract attention. Your images should work in harmony with the words on your website.

Video

Jack Straight From the Gut by Jack Welch – The story of Jack Welch, the former CEO of General Electric, tells how Welch helped turn GE into the powerhouse it is today.

Some say that, before too long, video will replace most other content on the Web. While I don't think that will happen any time soon, it is important to recognize video as a significant content element. It is also an element that is easy to do poorly. Because current technology makes it simple to make a video, you have to be careful that you don't just put anything up. Your video should be professional and match the other messages on your website.

Primary Website Text

Before there was a picture, there were 1,000 words to describe it.
–Corey Smith

Primary website content includes pages such as your homepage, about page, products and services page and contact page. These pages are the core of your website; it is your opportunity to discuss your primary brand messaging. This content will stay relatively static and will likely only be changed when your company's strategic direction changes. You should probably plan on updating this at least once per year, when you are getting ready to execute your annual business plan.

Blogs, Articles and News Stories

To most effectively attract visitors to your site and make it easily found by search engines, you'll want to have content that is continually updated. There is no easier way to do this than simply adding content such as blogs, articles and news stories on a regular basis.

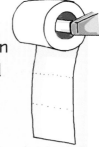

Nothing you read on blogs is considered real news.

BS Meter - 3/5

Comments

I am amazed at how many people don't realize that comments are content, too. Comments—such as those left via a Facebook profile—are driven by interesting content on your website. This allows website visitors to feel like they are a part of your decisions. But, a word of warning: be cautious with comments. If you don't manage them, spammers may take advantage of your commenting capabilities and try to direct your visitors to spammers' sites.

Discussion Forums

If you have a service with an active user base, a discussion forum is a great way to let your community talk with each other in a controlled environment. This type of forum works well in industries that require support (e.g. software companies or products requiring assembly); it's also useful when your brand becomes known for expertise, such as BodyBuilding.com. A discussion forum allows for a broad amount of content that you don't have to write, and it is good for website visitors as well as search engines. Just like with comments, be careful to watch for, and block, spammers.

WHERE DOES CONTENT BEGIN?

If content comes first, how do you start developing it? This is likely your key question right now. As the CEO, you are tasked with making sure it is done right for your site, and you probably need to be managing this more than doing it. However, if you are running a small business, you'll likely be the one to get this done. Whether you are building a website that will be 5 or 500 pages, the process is the same. The only difference is that one takes more time than the other. (Can you guess which one? Good, that's why you are the CEO.)

I'll give you the high-level steps here, but I have created a more specific documentation process on my website, http://coreysmith.ws.

Create a Succinct Message

Develop a succinct message of who you are. Make this a "tip of the spear" type of message, meaning that it is pointed and direct. While you'll be tempted to tell everyone about every service you offer, think of the auto mechanic. When you ask a mechanic what he does, he might say that he specializes in general engine repair. He won't say that he is a mechanic that fixes engines, carburetors, radiators and timing belts, changes oil, inspects fuel lines, checks differential fluid, replaces Johnson rods and…you get the point.

Get Organized

Start organizing your products and services into groupings that make sense. If you have been smart about how you have built your company, this should be reasonably easy as most companies are built with natural divisions of responsibility. If you are running Bob's Fish, Chips and Insurance, then you might have to get creative. Consider separating out the aspect of your business that is different and create a separate brand and website for that part. You can even sing the "one of these things is not like the other" song while you do it...unless you have a bad voice.

Decide What's Important

Decide what is important and what is not. This may be the hardest part, but try to think of this as a de-junking opportunity. You don't have to share everything that you do;

take the core of your business offerings and talk about that instead. It is better to have rich content about five offerings than weak content about ten. And, always make sure that everything comes back to your primary objective.

Outline Everything

Build an outline. This is just like writing an outline in school (sorry) and creating a hierarchy of how things should fit together. One way of doing this is by building a sitemap, and some people find that this is really the easiest way to go about outlining a site. If you think this might being easier for you, I have included instructions on this book's website as well.

The Creative Habit by Twyla Tharp – Tharp explores how to become more creative and effective with your creative materials. You must always seek and nurture inspiration to get the most out of yourself and your final product.

Group Your Offerings

Organize your page titles into a text document and start filling in content. This takes some time, but don't worry about creating the perfect first draft. Just get content out there. On some pages, you'll have too much and on others you'll have too little...that's okay, it's a start.

A site map (or sitemap) is a list of pages of a web site accessible to crawlers or users. It can be either a document in any form used as a planning tool for web design, or a web page that lists the pages on a web site, typically organized in hierarchical fashion

Correlate Your Content

As you are revising your content and working through your messaging, you'll start to see patterns emerge. You'll see where content starts to relate to other content, and you can annotate these places as links throughout your site. Don't worry about the technical way it will be done, just make note that they relate to each other.

Proofing, Proofing and More Proofing

Final proofing is important. As you do final proofing, make sure to ask people outside of your industry to read at least sections of your content to make sure you are speaking to the right audience. Hiring a proofreader for larger sites is a good idea, especially prior to implementation. On most modern websites, editing is easy, but it is much easier to fix the errors earlier in the process. However, be careful that you don't end up in a state of constant preparation; you should know when the content is "done".

Once the content is complete, you have now set the primary direction for your website. You have set the strategy, and everything needs to flow from this strategy. If the imagery doesn't match up, there will be a disconnect in the minds of your audience.

UNDERSTANDING YOUR AUDIENCE

In any medium (writing, advertising, etc.) it can be hard to remember who your audience is. When you don't speak to your audience, they don't listen...they simply turn off or go to another site

Mobile – More users than ever are accessing the Web through cell phones and tablets. Your website content needs to be readily available for these devices. Mobile sites are websites designed specifically for viewing on a mobile device.

Why would I pay to design a mobile site? No one uses their phones to surf the Web.

BS Meter – 4/5

> RSS – Really Simple Syndication. Literally. RSS allows your website visitors to subscribe to your content via an RSS reader or their email

that is speaking to them. Likewise, when designing and managing your website, one of the hardest things to do is remember who your audience is.

But, why is this so hard?

Oftentimes, this is hard because we want to write to people that are just like us. We tend to think of ourselves as the perfect audience, thinking that we know what our customers want to hear because we are just so smart. We have worked with them so long that we just naturally know what they are looking for. We are convinced that we know best.

Let me be blunt. You don't understand what your clients want to read like you think you do. Your audience has different needs than you do. You want to sell while they may or may not want to buy. This puts you in two distinctly different categories. The trick is learning how to speak to your customer, rather than to yourself. When you don't understand your audience, you lose all credibility.

Oftentimes, CEOs are so focused on running a business that they become disconnected from what clients really need. They tend to focus on selling widgets and forget to learn about their customer.

Don't get me wrong. I would never suggest that this is a condition endemic of any particular industry—it is a problem of just about every industry out there. You, however, have a unique opportunity to buck the trend and move ahead of your competition.

There are five main areas that your content must overcome (and possibly your sales reps need to overcome, too) when writing the content for your site.

Don't use jargon.

Every industry has its own vernacular. Since we are so accustomed to the way we talk in our given industry, it is easy to forget that clients don't live in our world. Chances are your clients don't do a Google search for your industry terms. In fact, most of them haven't even heard those terms. When writing or talking, make sure to you talk like they do.

You need the sale more than they do.

Sometimes this isn't true, but most of the time it is. You are probably trying to make your quota or hit your revenue numbers. Old school techniques of, "Buy now, because the price goes up tomorrow," are not nearly as effective as they used to be (in fact, they tend to backfire). Although it's a buzzword, consultative selling is what people want. They will buy from you when they know you understand their needs and that you have the knowledge and skill to perform. Your website is simply one way that you can show them that you understand them.

> When you don't understand your audience, you lose all credibility.
> – Corey Smith

Your clients aren't interested in what you are interested in.

You're clients aren't actively searching for case studies, articles and stories on your particular products. More often than not, they don't understand these things well enough to even know that they need to search. Instead of hitting them over the head with stats and figures, your website content must contain information they are interested in. The more interest you generate, the more likely customers are to understand and accept your message.

How much you care about what you have to say

VS.

How much others care about what you have to say

HOW MUCH THEY CARE

HOW MUCH YOU CARE

Content alone won't drive traffic.

Publishing content alone will not drive traffic to your site. If people aren't interested in your content, Google won't be interested either. It needs to be a concerted approach. We'll talk more about this in a later section on website traffic. For now, don't think that content will drive people to your site.

Customers don't understand all your services.

Your website is a great opportunity to cross-sell your other services. What percentage of your clients even know that you offer other products and services? How many problems do your clients face that you could solve today if they simply

Every CEO needs to understand how to wireframe, if only on paper. It allows for a more fluid method of communicating your vision.
– Corey Smith

knew you had the solution? If you drive your current customers to your website for one thing they want, you will have an opportunity to cross-sell your other items. But, be careful that you don't violate your primary objective.

As you think about your message, make sure that you understand who your audience is. Think back to the section on authenticity. Your brand is who you are, and this must be communicated with your customers.

> Wireframe —The most basic outline of your website. Your wireframe will include how the site will be laid out, but will not include any actual content other than section titles, layout of images and buttons.

THE WIREFRAME

With content in hand, you are ready to start designing. Now, don't get confused—I didn't say decorating, I said designing. When designing a house, you don't start with the paint; you start with the floor plan, the blueprint.

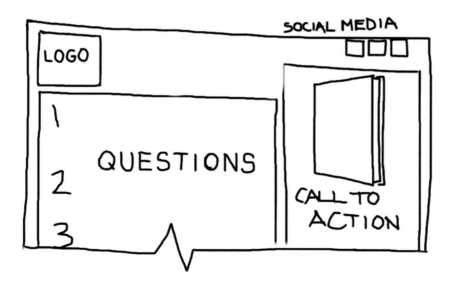

The wireframe of a website is the blueprint for everything else. Because you have created your outline or sitemap, you know how many pages you will have. You know what your objectives are and what you will say. Now it is time to figure out how it all fits together.

But, how will you know when your content is far enough along that you're able to move to the wireframe stage? That is a fair question. Sometimes, it is hard to envision what needs to be done before seeing how it is starting to come together. Because of this, I don't recommend that you completely finish the content before you start working on the wireframe. Rather, at this stage, think of content as a hybrid, ever-evolving aspect of the website. In fact, it is very beneficial if the content is written just before (or even concurrently with) the creation of the wireframe.

> When you know what your website should do, getting it to do that is much easier.
> – Corey Smith

Let me explain how this works; I'll use the analogy of writing this book.

As I am writing this book, I obviously have a lot of content to write and several elements are important. But, as I write this book, it is only text. The text, by itself, may be hard or boring to read (hopefully not). All of the other elements of the book give the text a deeper meaning. In addition, I don't know how much text I will need. If I am not cognizant of what I am writing, it could easily end up to be a 500-page book, and then you probably wouldn't be as interested in reading it. So, I write, then I design a little to see how it will fit together. Then, I write a little more, design a little more and see how it fits together.

The same approach can be used in building a website. Start with the content for the homepage as this is the most important landing page of your entire site. Once this is completed (remembering that it's still malleable), you will have already developed your succinct message. You should know who you are but probably haven't defined what you want people to do.

What should your website do?

This is when you decide what you want people to do on your site.

So, ask yourself this simple question: "What do I want my website to do?

From the content that you've written, you have talked about who you are and what your services are, but you haven't addressed what you want the visitors of your website to do.

Here are some possible answers:

- Sell some (or some more) products
- Generate warm leads
- Generate brand awareness
- Educate
- Offer customer service/support
- Include product demonstration

Whatever your answer is, it is important to know the answer so that you can properly implement it into your strategy.

In crafting the content for this call to action, think of it as your 30-second elevator pitch. Tell your customer what you want them to know, and how you'd like them to take action at the conclusion of this "conversation."

Like all forms of design, visual design is about problem solving, not about personal preference or unsupported opinion.
– Bob Baxley

If you were a designer, I'd talk to you about the various technical tools there are to wireframe your homepage; if you'd like to know, you can look at the resources section of my website. However, in my opinion, the most effective way to wireframe is to start with a white piece of paper and a Sharpie marker. On the white paper you simply draw a wireframe of how your website should be organized. In reality, it's the thickness of the marker that makes the difference. It prevents the first drafts from being over thought. (I'll make it even easier for you: the resources page of this book's website has downloadable pages with pre-drawn browser windows.)

When you have your first "thumbnails," and you feel pretty good about how it is coming together, then you can begin to refine them.

In the following pages, I have created a simple homepage. I started with a thumbnail, refined it a little and then finalized it. The final version of the wireframe should include all the content for the particular page.

DESIGN IS NOT ABOUT YOU

Wireframing is really about defining the image you want portrayed. At this point, we have not talked about the color or graphical side of your website but, instead, how people will interact. Just as with content writing, when you are defining (or redefining) your company's image, one of the most difficult tasks is to step back and understand who your real audience is.

Designing a logo, website, brochure or even something as simple as a blog post shouldn't elicit an attitude of, "I like it, so it is good."

I want an amazing website and I want it for under $200.

BS Meter – 4/5

The most important thing about any design is to remember your audience. Who are the people that you want to attract? Remember: at the end of the day, it is all about the customer.

Through this process of wireframing, you need to ask yourself who your audience is. Don't suppose that you know what your target audience needs more than they do. Ask members of your target audience, and then take their advice seriously. In the end, it really doesn't matter what you think.

> Whenever I see a bad logo, the first thought that goes through my mind is, "I Bet the CEO Designed that one."
> – Corey Smith

Asking for outside feedback and assistance can help make sure that you are writing and designing with the customer in mind. You'll have the opportunity to define how well you have done and modify the content before it hits the programming stage. In reality, the only hard part about it is setting your ego aside and focusing on the customer.

TIME FOR A LITTLE DECORATION

So, we have content. We have a wireframe. Let's add a splash of color. If you have used the documents that I provided on my website, you will have a pretty darn good strategy for your own site.

I am not going to take time to talk about how to make a website pretty; the designer that you delegate the task to knows about that. I am going to take time to help you identify what is pretty.

The challenge with design (graphical design) standards is that they change on a regular basis. The concept of Web 2.0 came about in 2004, and with it came very bubbly designs. This meant lots of rounded corners, glossy appearances and fading reflections. Around 2008, more and more designs started sporting a grunge look...so much so that a friend of mine was convinced that this was the latest trend and I should do the same. In the last year or so, Web graphics have become cleaner, with less rounded corners and a flatter appearance. However, it seems that we may be heading to a phase of richer colors and experiences as current technology allows more layering of colors and graphics.

> The two most important things in any endeavor are creativity and presentation.
> – Corey Smith

All of that doesn't matter to you since you aren't designing the graphical representation of your wireframe design. I only mention these trends to illustrate that graphical standards change. In fact, it doesn't take that long to see the standards shift. It may even seem like you only just made your site live when the next design trend starts to take over.

Your content and wireframe is there to set the requirements for the graphics. Your logo and brand colors help shape what your website should look like. Even though you will delegate the responsibility of creating the "decoration" of your website, you'll want to have a reasonable understanding of what is going on. Below, I lay out a simple process by which you can properly understand what you're looking for. Here are the five steps in the process:

Competitive Analysis

Look at as many of your competitors as you can. Look for the elements of their sites that you like and don't like. However, don't be the only one to analyze them. Pick your top five competitors and ask your friends and family to give you some feedback. I especially like to ask people that are outside my field because they will have a less biased opinion. Look at your competitors' sites and ask, "What are they trying to get me to do?" Then, assign a grade based on how well you think they are accomplishing their goal, and request the same of those you are asking for feedback from. This grade may be a bit arbitrary (e.g. 1-10) but it will allow you an opportunity to compare relative performance of your competitors.

General Design Research

Look at some of your favorite sites, preferably outside of your industry. Go on a hunt. Identify a number of sites and understand why you like them and what parts you like about them. Ask yourself the same question from step one, "What are they trying to get me to do?"

As with your competitive analysis, you'll want to grade your favorite websites with a relative grade (e.g. 1-10). You probably won't necessarily be looking at them from a perspective of what they are trying to get you to do because these favorite sites might be too different from your core business. However, if you find something compelling, be sure to take note of that.

Graphic Mockups

Start mocking up your site by creating pretty variations of your wireframe. This is where the designer gets a little bit of creative license. Talk with him or her about what you like and don't like. If you have the budget and time, create at least two different mockups and compare them against each other. These can be done in design programs such as Adobe Photoshop or Illustrator if you like. Some artists may even prefer to do the mockups directly in the Web browser, and there are some advantages

Wireframe

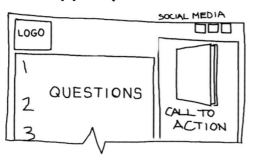

Mock Up

to that. Whichever way you choose to do it, make sure you have flexible options that you can consider and beat up.

Critically Analyze the Mockups

Look at the mockups and honestly compare them. Ask yourself if they fulfill your business requirements. Do they follow the strategy that you set forth? Don't let your artist take so much creative liberty that it changes your overarching strategy. You may need a few rounds of changes before you feel confident that you have accomplished what you are trying to accomplish, and it may take longer if your artist is "too creative," hasn't designed for the Web much before or if you haven't done a good job communicating your wishes. Above all, ask yourself and your advisors, "How does this adhere to our primary objective?"

Elicit Feedback

When you feel that you have one or two mockups that you really like—mockups that embody your brand identity, illustrate your primary and secondary calls to action and meet all of your business requirements—then you are ready to have your ego bruised again. It's time to ask people you know to give their honest feedback. This means customers, strangers, random people on the Internet...no one is safe from your solicitation for feedback. Make sure that you are willing to make suggested changes if it takes you closer to your primary objective. I'll talk about testing tools near the end of the book, and you'll learn about the various tools you can use to make your testing a bit easier.

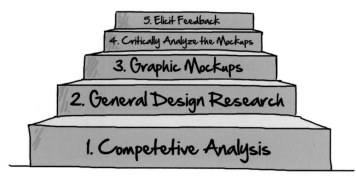

The 5 Step Website Design Process:

5. Elicit Feedback
4. Critically Analyze the Mockups
3. Graphic Mockups
2. General Design Research
1. Competetive Analysis

BRINGING IT ALL TOGETHER

With content in hand, wireframes that show your layout and pretty graphics that make your website look like raindrops and lollipops, you're ready to give your website programmers the go-ahead to starting building the site.

Remember the Disneyland analogy? It applies here, too. Before the first shovel ever hit the ground, Walt and his team defined where everything was going to go. They knew the waterways, the paths and that a bathroom would be around the corner from the shooting gallery in Adventureland. They knew where the stores would go and where the cast members would exit the park to go on break. They had their plan in place.

After the plan was in place, they were ready to start digging and building. It is reasonable to assume that decisions needed to be made throughout the process of building Disneyland Park because they couldn't have foreseen everything. However, those decisions were made easier because the planning process (strategy phase) allowed them a clear map of how, when and where to do what, allowing them to progress, despite small hiccups.

Likewise, a good strategy and thorough design will help you avoid costly delays in the implementation (programming) phase of your site. It will help your content match your graphics while helping the site achieve its goal (whatever that may be). If problems do arise, your clearly laid plans will aid in quickly overcoming small issues, getting the project back on track and staying within budget.

We won't take time in this book to talk about what it takes to actually build your website because, as mentioned before, the actual building of your site is tactical fulfillment. Your job is to set the vision, help ensure the strategy is on track and give your team the opportunity to make your vision a reality.

Web Marketing

THE POWER OF VOICE

In 1933, Adolf Hitler came to power in Germany, first as Chancellor under a lame duck president, then as Führer. The man who brought Hitler to power, Joseph Goebbels, was the real messenger for Hitler's vitriol. Starting in 1926, Goebbels produced significant propaganda with messages that vilified ethnic Jews, socialists and liberals. In 1933, a new office in Hitler's cabinet was created for Goebbels and he was appointed Reich Minister of Public Enlighten- ment and Propaganda.

Goebbels was almost cynical in his view of propaganda. He wrote, "That propaganda is good which leads to success, and that is bad which fails to achieve the desired result. It is not propaganda's task to be intelligent, its task is to lead to

success." He felt that the primary purpose of propaganda was to persuade others to the author's point of view. In fact, he felt that it didn't even have to be smart, just effective.

While Hitler's Germany was marching across Europe, Americans did not have the desire to enter into another war across the Atlantic. Many members of the United States government, including President Roosevelt, understood that entering the war would be important. Because of this, in the late 1930s, the United States began its own propaganda efforts, urging Americans to assist by doing things as simple as buying defense bonds, later called war bonds.

It wasn't until the attack on Pearl Harbor on December 7, 1941, that Americans began to agree that something must be done. It was then that American propaganda began in earnest.

The real challenge that American propaganda faced was that the population was guarded about being told what to believe. They had their fill of propaganda during World War I. However, this new war seemed no longer comfortably distant. It was no longer a war that was simply in a far off land. As such, it was much easier for these messages to take hold.

There was a distinct difference in the messages of German and American propagandists. Germany controlled all messages that the populace heard, and Goebbels only allowed messages that helped convince the German people that other races were inferior and that Hitler's (Goebbels's) view of Germany was correct. Because of Goebbels's cynicism, he felt that the people weren't smart enough to think for themselves and would blindly believe his messages as long as any opposition was censored. In America, on the other hand, the primary purpose of propaganda was to help the war effort, thereby defending American freedom. The messages were primarily of patriotism, work ethic and unity in the face of a tyrannical foe. American propaganda did not supplant other messages or censor opposition; it spoke to the hearts and minds of the American populace.

One other key difference was that German artwork, music and other types of propaganda were driven by Hitler's regime under the direction of Goebbels. In America, the majority of the propaganda was produced as a volunteer effort among artists, television producers, moviemakers and even private corporations. Companies such as General Motors, Lucky Strike and Coca-Cola encouraged the general population by showing what they were doing to support the war effort.

American propaganda was truly a grass roots movement. In fact, in today's vernacular, we could consider that most of the messages became viral. It allowed the American people to be a part of the war effort in both major and minor ways. They could do great things like build battleships and tanks in shipyards and factories. They could also do small things like save grease from their cooking for use in making bombs or plant a garden to help avoid a food shortage. Slogans such as "loose lips sink ships" and "eat what you can and can what you can't" became part of the American lexicon.

> Propaganda – Information that is used to promote a particular point of view. Propaganda is changing beliefs, whereas marketing is changing habits and action.

Without the backing of the American people, there is no way that the Allies would have overcome the Axis powers. It was through propaganda that the American people felt that unity was a reality and that they were fighting against one, common foe.

> *Neuromarketing: Understanding the Buy Buttons in your Customers Brain* by Patrick Renvoise – This book will help you discover the most effective techniques to communicate with your customers and craft powerful messaging.

INFLUENCING THE CROWD

The primary goal of propaganda is to change hearts and minds. While we generally do not consider marketing to be a form of propaganda, the marketer's job is the same—to change a customer's heart and mind. And, most advertisers are only working to change minds, forgetting the heart component; this is one key reason why German propaganda was not as effective as American propaganda during World War II.

Understanding the basis for offline marketing helps us to understand how to market online. By evoking emotion in our marketing efforts, we are able to generate the strongest reaction in our target audience...and, hopefully, win customers over. An advertising message that tells you how to think is never as effective as a message that speaks to your current beliefs and values, causing you to feel a connection to the message. Even today, the best advertisements are those that speak to who you already are and what you already believe.

Begin with Why by SImon Sinek – Simon Sinek explores why some individuals and organizations are more innovative, influential, and profitable than others. There are many questions to ask in business, but you must start with "why."

During World War II, posters were the single most common tactic used in American propaganda, with 200,000 different designs produced during the war. What made World War II propaganda successful was the stories behind the posters and the emotional link the stories created with the viewer. The strongest messages were those that evoked emotion in the audience. Movies, newsreels and radio were very powerful, but posters were also able to target feelings of pride, emotional and physical strength and support for those fighting overseas. The propaganda would have made no difference if there had been little or no emotion tied to it.

All online marketing needs to use the same approach of effective story telling. One of the challenges in online marketing is the idea that technology can limit our story telling abilities because we tend to think that we have to understand the technology before we can tell a story. In fact, it is the opposite. The interactive possibilities online provide you with virtually limitless opportunities to tell your story and affect the hearts and minds of your audience. Interactivity, for website visitors, can be as simple as allowing them to comment on your posts. This allows them the opportunity to engage with the authors of the stories to ask questions and add their own perspectives.

Regardless of how interactive your website is, story telling will allow you to create an image in your visitors' minds that will help them see who you are and what you believe. As we discuss online marketing throughout this section, we'll spend a bit more time on how to use effective story telling in your marketing.

LOCATION, LOCATION, LOCATION

Perhaps the most effective way to understand how the Web fits with conducting business online is to compare it to a brick and mortar establishment. As we talk about these concepts, I want you to think back to the Foundational Approach to Web Marketing (Section 1). The basis or foundation of your Web marketing is your website. We'll use a storefront as an analogy to your website. In the previous section of the book, we talked about Web presence, focusing on the primary presence, your website.

A website is the equivalent of a store located on Main Street of Anytown, USA. Whether it's a bakery, pet store or apothecary, you have a store.

Your primary objective for that store is to sell your wares, because you can't stay in business if you don't sell your stuff. In today's environment, we think of using online advertisements to get people to come to a website. I want to put that out of your mind for a moment, because I want you to understand how it's been done for thousands of years…and, more importantly, that online and offline marketing really aren't that different.

When we think about selling our goods offline, we think of billboards, signs, radio, television, yellow pages…the list goes on and on. In a brick and mortar store, we even think about displays, impulse items, how the register is positioned and how we

When I hear a stupid jingle and comment on it, someone invariably will say, "You may not like it, but you remember them." Just because I know who they are doesn't mean that I'll want to buy from them.
- Corey Smith

interact with our customers. But, when we think of these options, we may be unsure of how they actually drive consumer behavior. Most storeowners just know that there are all these things that we need, but they don't really think strategically about how to sell them. There are a list of tactics they just try to accomplish, and they'll usually try as many as possible until they figure out what really works.

To better understand this, I'm going to break it down into three levels: brand awareness, traffic generation and conversion. Without forgetting that the primary objective is to sell things at the cash register, it's important to remember that just because you have a store, it doesn't mean that people will come.

Storefront Brand Awareness

The first thing we want to do with our storefront is get some brand awareness. We might set up a sign out front for passersby, pass out fliers or do some radio advertisement. Once this awareness is generated, you are partway there.

Brand awareness is very misunderstood. Many people expect that once brand awareness has been generated, people will come in and buy. This is not so. Think back to our story at the beginning of the book about the Vin Fiz Grape Drink. Just because the company had brand awareness, it didn't cause people to drink their soda. Brand awareness needs to be pretty compelling in order for people to take action on it alone.

Storefront Traffic Generation

Because brand awareness does not guarantee that people will come into the store, we have to look for ways to generate traffic. The tactics for generating traffic are often implemented so poorly that they don't generate traffic at all. Radio, television and even simple door-to-door fliers, while they try to get people in the door, almost always fall into the category of brand awareness. What distinguishes your tactic as a traffic generator is having a clear call to action— a clear message that tells your audience what to do.

In our storefront example, let's assume that you pass out fliers, have a radio ad and even have a big sign that says, "Buy now! Get 10% off!" All advertisements provide brand awareness, but when you have a clear call to action, it becomes traffic generation.

Storefront Conversions

Getting people into your store doesn't mean they will buy. Getting a person to buy is known as a conversion. There are many factors that go into getting people to buy, although it's usually assumed that it comes down to one thing...price. Most people think that if your price is the lowest, people will naturally buy. But selling stuff is more than price, and the Disneyland example illustrates

this well. In the beginning, getting in Disneyland was only $1.00. At $1.00 per ticket, they didn't generate enough revenue to pay for even the basics of operation. Traffic alone did not mean that Disneyland made any money at all; they made their money through requiring people to buy tickets for rides, as well as offering merchandise and concessions. If you've been to any Disney property, you know that everything is set up to allow you to relieve your pockets of additional weight. Effective businesses spend time, money and effort to optimize their stores to make it easiest for people to buy.

Online Brand Awareness (Search Engine Optimization)

Now , how do we relate this to the Web? By this point, you should have completed all of the steps in Section 2 to create a compelling Web presence. This is where we really get into the crux of the Foundational Approach to Web Marketing introduced in the first section of the book. Brand awareness for your website begins with search engine optimization (SEO), which starts the process of people knowing who you are. When they search for your services online in Google, Bing, or other search engines, SEO helps you sit higher in the search results. It's akin to your sign on the street being more prominent...or, more aptly, other people putting up signs for you that point to your store.

Online Traffic Generation

Getting people to come to your store offline is similar to generating traffic online. When you buy an ad online, send out email marketing, have conversations in social media or include your URL on your business card, you are generating traffic. As with your offline traffic tactics, your online tactics can also generate brand awareness. Most of these traffic generators also help your search engine rankings to some degree, similar to the way that offline traffic generation tactics help to generate brand awareness.

Conversion – Getting someone to do something you want (e.g. go to another page, fill out a lead form or buy something).

Conversion Rate - The percentage of people that do the thing you want versus those that don't.

Conversion Rate Optimization - Making changes on your website that help increase your conversion rate.

Online Conversions

When people come to your website, as with the brick and mortar store, there is no guarantee they'll do what you want. Just like in a store, buying something online is called a conversion. This can be broadened to say that getting users to do anything you want them to do on your website is called a conversion. It could be selling something. It could be filling out a form to give you a lead. It could even be as simple as going to the next page. Getting better at getting them to do what you want them to do is called conversion rate optimization (CRO).

In the coming sections, we'll talk more about these three main components of Web marketing: search engine optimization (SEO), traffic generation and conversion rate optimization (CRO). These three components are what make Web marketing work. They build on the foundation of your Web presence and make it work for you .

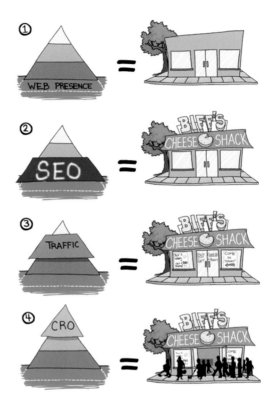

CREATING "EVERGREEN" SEO

Search engine optimization (SEO) is simply the process of getting your website to appear at the top of the search engines. There is a reason that marketing your website starts with search engine optimization. It is the same reason why you would start marketing your storefront with brand awareness—if your customers don't know you exist, they won't buy from you.

Some consultants talk about starting with social media or paid advertisements, but search engines are where potential clients are already looking, and it is a very cost-effective way to start. More importantly, if you use search engine optimization to generate placement in the search engines, you'll continue to reap the reward of that work long after you stop working on it. You may choose to jump directly to traffic generation to get an immediate boost, but you should never ignore search engine optimization.

SEO –Search Engine Optimization - SEO is the process of getting your site listed at the top of search engines. SEO is not a one time event, and must be maintained to achieve the most effective results.

One way to see how well you are doing is to Google yourself . Companies should regularly do this to see how well they rank in the search engines.

I've heard it said that buying ads is like renting a house, while performing SEO is like buying a house. It develops equity. If done properly, it can be a year or more before someone unseats you from the top of the search engine.

You have to be careful, though. Search engine optimization is not a traffic generation tactic, per se. It is the equivalent of brand awareness, because enough brand awareness will generate traffic. Keep this in mind as we talk about search engine optimization. I'll go into greater detail about traffic generation in a later discussion.

If we look back at our example of the storefront, there are certain things that have to be done first. The store has to be built right and be inviting to customers. But, we also have to be sure that street signage does its best to draw attention, without being gaudy or distracting to those trying to decide where to buy. It is the same with websites—they should be functional and welcoming, but not overdone.

There are only three key components to search engine optimization, which we'll examine together.

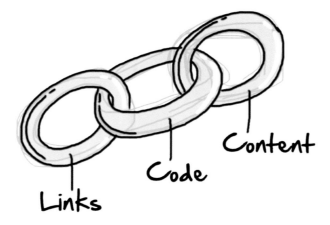

Links

Code

Content

Content

Content is the single most important part of your search engine optimization efforts. In fact, it is the single most important part to how your website will function for users. We talked before about the various types of content in your website. It can be text, images, video, audio and comments, among others. Search engines understand content. They understand text the best, but if you've added descriptions and tags, they'll even know what an image or video is about. You might think that I am talking about content too much or going overboard trying to make a point. However, it bears repeating: content is important to your Web presence, as well as your ongoing search engine optimization.

Links

When other sites link to your website, they act as votes for the search engines. When you have links coming in, it's as if the other websites are saying that they deem you as reliable. Search engine optimizers (professionals that perform search engine optimization) place a great deal of emphasis on the number of links and, if they are good, the quality of links that come into the websites they manage. These are called inbound links. You can link all you want within your site or to other websites, but it's the

Link Equity – A measurement of your inbound links based on number, as well as the authority of the sites linking to you. A link from a major corporation's site means a lot more than one from Crazy Uncle Ted's Wordpress blog that has been around for less than a month.

Inbound Links – Also known as Backlinks. These are links coming into a website from an outside source. These links are very important in SEO (Search Engine Optimization), as they act as a recommendation from another site.

Outbound Links – A link from your website to another. Search Engines view these as sites you are recommending to your visitors.

inbound links that matter. We will not talk about specific link building tactics because the most effective methods change often. Generally speaking, however, highly compelling content and activity in social media will generate the highest quality of inbound links.

Code

The code, or the way your website is built, is also very important. The way the code is created, including the hidden descriptors (tags and attributes) of the page, images, video and other content, makes a big difference in how the website is read by the search engines. Usually, bad code won't detract from your rankings, but it may not help. Of course, there are techniques to try to fool the search engines into thinking your website is something it is not...though those techniques will certainly hurt your chances as search engines are getting much better at discovering them. Since we are not going to talk about the tactics of developing good code, my best council is to make sure that you thoroughly interview the programmers for your website, ask for references and perhaps even use a consultant to ensure that you hire the right person, team or company.

MEASURE & ADJUST

I talk with clients all the time about ways to optimize their websites for increasing traffic. Often, I get the question, "Well, can I just optimize my website now? Then, in a year, I can optimize it again?"

The short answer is, "No."

Search engine optimization is not a one-time event. It isn't something that you do once and never look back on. It requires evolving content.

This evolving content provides the search engines with new pages and new content to index on your website. It provides visitors with options to search for.

> I can't change the direction of the wind, but I can adjust my sails to always reach my destination.
> –Jimmy Dean

The reality is, you never know how people will find you. You never know what search terms they use. For example, on my old, out-of-date business and technology blog, one of the most commonly searched terms that led people to my site was, "Dear Valued Customer." As of the writing of this book, my blog is still listed as number three on the Google search results. I don't know why people search on Google for those words. I don't know if they are looking for a form letter they can send to their clients or if they are looking for something else. The point is, I would never have guessed that people would find me based on that search, but because I had so much constantly evolving content, I had people finding me daily that wouldn't have found me otherwise. This is a testament to the everlasting nature of search engine optimization as I have not been active on that website in quite some time.

Search engine optimization is a constantly moving target. If you think that it is something you can do today and not touch for a year or two, you will be missing out on a lot

of traffic. As you are sitting and waiting for your potential clients to come and find you, your competitors are working to provide search engines with more, varied content to index and feed searchers. Once your site it optimized, you can take a breath for a moment or work on the next set of terms, but getting there takes time and consistency.

The question I get quite often is, "Well, isn't SEO some magical thing that only really smart people know how to do?" (Okay, I paraphrased a little.) True, there are some components that make it a little more complicated to understand...after all, that is why SEOs (search engine optimizers) charge up to $15,000 or more for a relatively small website just to optimize website content...once. Then, they'll usually charge a hefty monthly fee to make sure that the website stays optimized; after all, SEO is not a one-time event.

Search engine optimization is something that needs to be continually addressed. Not only does a website need to have new content added all the time, but the existing, static content needs to be adjusted, changed and modified. Moreover, think beyond the search engines and consider the website visitor—if your website isn't evolving with new, compelling stories, then why in the world would someone ever come back?

A Traffic Generation tactic that doesn't generate traffic is simply a brand awareness tactic.
– Corey Smith

When you sell items in your store (offline or online), you may be able to get some repeat business from people who need replacements. If you have a product that only needs to be replaced once in a very long while, like a flagpole, then you can expect that your visitors won't return very often. So, new items and offerings can greatly increase the traffic from existing customers, and it is the same with website content. A search engine's goal is to return relevant results; if your content is compelling to people, it will also be compelling to search engines.

The Latest Craze

Before we get too deep into the three tactics, I should probably address something specific. While these three primary tactics haven't changed too significantly over the last few years, they have become more prominent. Ever has it been, however, that advertising companies have always tried to get their clients to focus on the services that they provide. For example, if the sales rep provides radio advertising, then that is the best way to advertise.

Over the last few years, advertisers have been moving online; because of this, new tactics have entered the mix. With all of the new advertising options available, there is a tendency to think that offline ads no longer work. While there may be some truth in that, the reality is that just because it's online, it doesn't mean it will work and just because it's offline doesn't mean it won't.

When marketing, either online or offline, be careful to avoid looking at marketing as a series of checklists. Yes, understanding the tactics is important to setting the strategy, but avoid jumping on the latest tactic just because an advertiser suggests it.

HOW TO GENERATE TRAFFIC

Just because a website has great stories, the best content and people are able to identify with its message, it does not mean that people will find it. And, just because you are found high in search engine results, there is no guarantee that people will come running (or surfing) to your site.

Who is your online market?

The most obvious answer is, "anyone online." However, that may be a bit over simplified. I think the better answer is, the people that are online looking for your products.

Not long ago, I bought dog training from a company based on their sign on the side of the road... never looked online because I assumed they wouldn't market that way.

When talking to the trainer, he said that signs on the road were at least ten times more cost effective than online advertising.

In the coming years that will shift. Each industry will have varying levels of success.

So, the real question is, "How long will you take before you finally figure it out?"

When it comes down to it, even though the primary purpose of SEO is to be at the top of the search engines, the main reason is to generate traffic. When you dominate search engines with the terms that people are searching, it will naturally generate traffic to your site. However, the real problem with search engine optimization is that you don't necessarily know what people are searching for and clicking on. You could spend hours writing a story that you think will drive the masses to your site and nothing will happen. But then a user will write one pithy comment as a backhanded compliment, and it will go viral.

Because of this, traffic requires a bit of thought. Search engine optimization is still important, and it allows your content to be found long term. In fact, if you write lots of stories and publish them in several locations, you can be found in multiple positions at the top of Google. The more listings you have at the top of the search engines, the greater the chance of garnering traffic to your website. If you are careful to analyze the way people are coming to your site through the analytic reports (available through most Web hosting services), you can even know what terms to focus on and what generates traffic.

The most important thing to understand about generating traffic from search engine optimization is that it can take time. You first have to get to the top, and then you have to analyze it to see what is getting the results you want. In the short term, other forms of traffic generation become your keys to success. With that in mind, radio, television, fliers and billboards can be considered traffic generation tactics. In fact, even your business card and sales people can be tactics to drive traffic to your website.

For the purposes of this book, we are going to focus on online traffic generation. Even with focusing on generating traffic online, we aren't going to talk about all the options you have for generating traffic. We'll just focus on the top three tactics:

- Social media
- Paid placement (PPC, banner ads)
- Email marketing

It's important for you, as the CEO, to understand these three primary tactics so that you can understand what the options are for your business. If you can only do one, then you'll have a basic understanding of each to help make a more educated decision.

TRAFFIC GENERATION: SOCIAL MEDIA

 circle of influence.

circle of life.

 ring of fire.

Over the last few years, social media has grown in popularity. I mention this first because social media is currently the fastest growing online marketing tactic. Everyone is trying to figure out how to make money from Twitter, Facebook and the multiple other social media outlets there are. I don't know if there is a week that goes by that I don't get an invite to participate in some new social network that is designed to be perfect for the way I do things.

The social media platforms that are quickly gaining traction among users are location based services such as Foursquare.com and Gowalla.com. They allow people to "check-in" with their smartphone to a physical location. This allows the visitors of a physical location post online where they are.

Not long ago, a business consultant mentioned to me, "I need to help my client build a social media strategy."

I thought that was a very odd question, so I said, "Tell me about this company's social strategy."

I received a blank stare because, of course, they did not have a social strategy for their company... that would simply be absurd.

The operative word in social media is social. It means that we need to be social in order for social media to make sense. After all, social media's primary objective is to facilitate conversation. Its purpose is not to help you make money or sell your widgets. Don't get me wrong—there will be plenty of opportunities to sell online and

> Location Based Services (LBS) – These are a form of social media that are based on your location. Using a service such as Foursquare or Gowalla, people "check-in" to a physical location. Location based services attempts to tie social media with your physical location to generate traffic and additional brand awareness.

through social circles. You'll have more than enough chances to pitch your product to those in your circles of influence.

Let's compare social media as a networking event filled with people. At this event, you'll have varying levels of familiarity with the attendees, from those you know very well to those that you don't know at all.

Imagine, if you will, walking up to people, shaking their hands and saying, "Hello, my name is George, and I can get you a deal on cell phones. I have a special running today."

Unfortunately, that is what happens all too often in social media. Businesses start by becoming acquaintances with people, then immediately begin to pitch their products.

Social media is an opportunity to talk to several people in a much shorter period of time than it would take to talk in person. Because social media's purpose is to facilitate conversation, it is important to start with a conversation that is meaningful to the people with whom you are talking. It is through those conversations that relationships are formed; it is from those relationships that transactions occur.

Another assumption to get past in social media is the idea that you have to understand the technology. In fact, it's the hardest misconception to get past in online marketing in general. The tendency is to think that, because the technology is different, the way marketing has been conducted for the last 100 years is somehow ineffective or that this new method will take way too much time. Rather, online marketing is just an extension of the marketing you already know.

Google+ is the most recent social project from Google that launched in June of 2011. Google+ combines features from multiple other social networks, in an attempt to do them better. (according to Google)

The real challenge with social media, for the beginner, is the fact that it's new, not that it's techy. It always takes time to develop a comfort level with new things; it takes even longer for things that seem difficult or that we don't see the immediate value in. Social media, just like anything new, is something that requires a commitment of time in which you develop a process that works for you.

So, what should you do with social media? How do you get your business involved and make it effective for you?

The most important first step is to be willing to experiment. Everyone's experience will be different, and it may take some time to find the path that works for you. Many people seem to think that, because technology is involved, there is a science of steps that must be taken to sell online. That isn't really true—the only "science" is in the following steps:

- Post messages that are relevant to your audience.
- Find people you like and follow them.
- Comment on other people's posts.
- Genuinely work to build relationships.

Everything else is dependent on your skills in developing conversations. It's dependent on you being social.

So, how does social media generate traffic? After all, the real point isn't to make lasting friendships; it's to grow a business. Social media generates traffic by people acting on recommendations made by people they know. Telling stories through social media allows people to want to share those stories with others. It is the same as the American propaganda at the beginning of this section. The stories they told were compelling, and people participated in activities like victory gardens or cutting back on sugar to help the war effort. The more compelling you are in your conversations, the more likely people will be to take action on what you have to say. The more interesting you are, the more they will do what you ask them to do (buy something, submit a lead, etc).

I would like to add one thing about social media. Of all the traffic generation tactics, social media is the one that helps in search engine optimization the most. Remember how we talked about inbound links as one of the tactics for advancing in the search engines? Well, every time you post a link on a social media site, it tells the search engines that there is value in what you have to say. However, as helpful as social media is with search engine optimization, its real value is in helping you build meaningful relationships with your clients.

TRAFFIC GENERATION: PAID PLACEMENT

Paid advertising has been around for as long as media has been available to charge for it—print, radio, television and now online. The traditional approach to paid advertisement has been to pay per the number of viewers. I like to think of it as cost per eyeballs. Each advertiser (TV, radio, etc.) will have a different name for this, but the philosophy is the same: the more we shout at people, the more they will take action.

This is a decent approach if the goal is brand awareness. Ask your radio rep or television advertiser how much traffic you'll get from their work and they will never be able to give you a number.

Generally speaking, paid online advertising is meant to drive traffic; it's not just a method of brand awareness like an offline ad might be. Minimally, if it doesn't drive traffic, it should certainly help with brand awareness, but it won't help with getting ranked higher in the search engines.

Paid advertising has two approaches. The first is to pay per impression, meaning each time the ad appears; this

If we pay for 1000 impressions, we don't know if we are paying for 1000 people viewing one, 100 people viewing 10 times, or 1 person viewing 1000 times.
– Corey Smith

is equivalent to the concept of cost per eyeballs. With most banner advertising, you will pay a flat fee for your ad to be shown for a certain number of assumed or actual impressions. I say assumed because it is usually sold based on how many impressions the site has had in the past, and sites simply estimate what it will be in the future based on past performance. If your ad gets no one to click on it, then you still pay the same fee you would if thousands of people click on the ad and make your website crash.

The more favored approach for paid placement is pay-per-click, also referred to as PPC. This is advertising that you only pay for if someone actually clicks on the link. The best-known example of this is the ads on a Google search results page, which are marked as sponsored results. These ads also commonly appear on Facebook pages. PPC is a popular choice because you only pay for results—if no one clicks your link, you don't pay anything. You can't get that type of guarantee in any other form of advertising. With PPC, you only pay when traffic is actually driven to your site.

Generally, PPC works better in an environment where the advertising targets viewers by aligning with their interests. In the Google search results, PPC ads are based on the search terms people are looking for. Try it now, go to Google.com and search for a term such as frogs. Look at the ads; noticed that they are related to frogs. Now, go to your Facebook page (if you have one). Assuming you don't have an ad blocker, you should see ads based on your interests. This is done by analyzing your profile, conversations and friends to provide you with ads that are hopefully more relevant to you. So, for example, if you've been posting about your upcoming trip to Hawaii, you might see vacation deals to Maui. Lately, websites (such as Google and Facebook) are letting users rank ads, further personalizing the advertising experience.

> PPC – AKA Pay Per Click Advertising. Instead of paying a flat rate for an advertisement, pay per click means you only pay when users click on your advertisement and go to your page.

TRAFFIC GENERATION: EMAIL MARKETING

From the moment that marketers figured out how to collect email addresses, email marketing has been a very popular approach to marketing online. Many people assume that email marketing means spamming people; after all, so many of us have received so much spam in our inboxes over the years. In fact, some people may even assume that email marketing is not very effective because nobody likes unwanted messages.

Consider this: if email marketing is ineffective, why do you receive spam messages? What's the use in sending an email if there isn't a return on the investment? Clearly, the spammers are getting something out of it.

Landing Pages – Also known as a Lead Capture Page. This is the page that appears in response to clicking on an advertisement or promotion on the web. Always remember that your home page will always be your most important landing page.

Email marketing is very effective if done right, but it is easy to do wrong. Most businesses that use online services such as Constant Contact and iContact don't realize that they are actually spamming their clients. The true definition of spam is sending mass messages from an electronic system to people who don't want that message. While the law is reasonably loose on what is called spam, most email systems are very strict on how they define spam. Therefore, if you are even perceived to be a spammer, they'll block you first and let you defend yourself later.

WEB MARKETING

Now comes the question: "How can I do email marketing if there is a possibility of getting shut down?"

I'll answer that question by explaining the two parts of email marketing that you need to be aware of: creating the message and managing your audience.

Creating the Message

When creating a message for an email marketing campaign, the process and requirements are virtually identical to that of creating a website. When planning your message, there are three components that you need to consider before you send: purpose, content and code.

Email Purpose

You might have many purposes for your email marketing message. The purpose is effectively your primary objective, so you should narrow it down to one primary and one or two secondary goals. It could be that you just want to update your audience with information about what you are up to, or you might want to send out daily or weekly specials. In order to properly define the purpose, you need to understand your audience and what they expect. If they signed up for your email, then you can be a bit more verbose. However, if you have taken your marketing

You need to choose either Web or Traditional Marketing. There is no point in investing in both.

BS Meter - 4/5

list and just moved them to your email database, then the message needs to be so simplified that they don't assume that you are just spamming them.

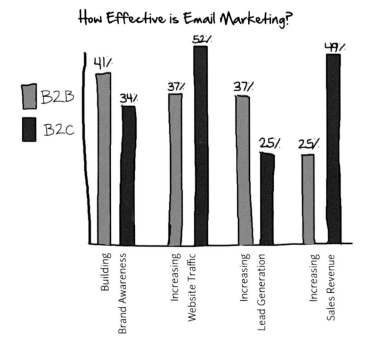

How Effective is Email Marketing?

Content

Content is the real key to your success in email marketing, just as it is in the other areas of Web marketing. There are two parts to the content in your email. The first part is the subject line. This is what will, hopefully, get people to open your email. It needs to be compelling and tested for success. After all, if people don't open your email, they will never see your message. The second part is the content of the message. This is where you educate, inform and get your message across. You'll want to have color, graphics and well-worded copy. This is also where you have the call to action. If your purpose is a daily specials email, then you can include a strong pitch. If your purpose is education, then your call to action should probably be in a sidebar and less obvious.

Code

The code is what will allow your email to be visible. If you use an emailing service, such as Constant Contact or iContact, then use their templates to build your email. Whether you have someone build it or you use a template provided by the service provider, test that email in as many email clients (Outlook, Web Mail, Mac Mail, etc.) as you can, as they all render appearances differently. Also, don't get carried away with the design. Because of the difference in the way email clients view emails and load images, it may look great on your computer, but you want to ensure that it looks good everywhere else as well. Simple is the name of the game in email marketing composition.

Audience Management

In my opinion, I think that audience management is the hardest part about email marketing. Depending on your purpose and messaging, your audience will start to get tired of hearing from you at some point. A daily fitness update sent to people wanting to be fit will have more longevity than a heavy equipment manufacturer trying to elicit interest in tractors.

Because of this, the first part of audience management is message management... so, make sure you are telling compelling stories. Remember, stories don't have to be monolithic diatribes, and they should not be self-serving. They do, however, have to be compelling to your audience. If your content is compelling enough, it will grow organically as your audience shares the information with their friends.

When you are ready to market consistently via email, you'll want to start building your list. This list should come from your personal and sales contacts, and it should be from prospects that have said they'd be interested in your emails. One very effective way to gain emails is from trade shows and conventions; just make sure people know that you are going to add them to your list so they are not surprised.

A common way to build your email database is to look at your current client list. You can begin by sending them a quick note asking if they want to receive your regular communication. I like this approach because it avoids disrespecting them by just starting to send them a large volume of messages; it is important that you don't jump into this in a way that will jeopardize your relationships. Just remember, if you ask for their permission to market to them, you'll want to be prepared that they may say no.

I do have one word of caution. There are many list providers (companies that will sell you a list of emails) that will claim that their list is opt-in or perfect for your market. They'll use terms like "100% opted-in emails" or "trusted email lists". The reality is that most people do not knowingly give permission to have their addresses sold. Typically, a box is accidentally left checked on an online form, allowing the addresses to be sold. The point? They don't want your emails, and they didn't opt-in to your weekly newsletter. Buying email lists is very expensive and will never be as effective as collecting the emails yourself.

THE USER EXPERIENCE

What's the point of having a website if it isn't useful to visitors? Earlier, we talked about search engine optimization driving up your rankings and how that doesn't guarantee traffic. Then, we discussed three distinct traffic generation tactics: social media, pay-per-click and email marketing. However, getting people to come to your website will not make them do what you want them to do (convert). Think back to our store-

How much should you spend on marketing?

There is no definitive answer. The short answer is you should spend as much as it takes to accomplish your business objectives, but not more. Most companies that have a large marketing budget spend the greatest percentage of their budget in paid advertising placement.

You'll want to research the standards in your industry and consider what type of growth you are looking for. Most low-growth industries can spend as little as .5% of revenue and medium to high growth industries can spend more than 10% of revenue. Whatever you choose, your marketing message needs to speak to who you really are and not to who you want people to believe you are.

front analogy; just because people walk into your store, and even browse for hours, they will not necessarily buy.

If you optimize your website's usability , you will find that people will do more of what you want more often. Usability, in its simplest terms, is how easy it is for a user to know what to do, where to find things and, most importantly, how to give you money. When talking about usability, several things come into play, including functionality, interaction, dynamic content and Web standards.

> Making the simple complicated is commonplace; making the complicated simple, awesomely simple, that's creativity.
> – Charles Mingus

Functionality

Functionality is the combination of common sense and viability. When considering a website's functionality, think of it as the most obvious way it should be used. Let's take this a step further and compare it to a door. If a door has a standard doorknob, you know which way to push or pull after the knob is turned. If there is a long, bar-like handle across the door, you may not have a clue where to push. I can't tell you how often I push on a door in a public place, only to find that I pushed on the wrong side of the handle. Just like the first door, a well designed website should be easy to use, and a visitor shouldn't have to guess what to do or how to find information.

Above the Fold – The portion of a Web page that is seen without having to scroll. This is where the primary content that you want readers to see goes. If its below the fold, there is no guarantee your readers will ever scroll to it.

Interaction

The more you allow your website visitors to interact, the longer they'll stay and the more likely they are to connect to your message.

Allowing commenting on blog posts and discussion forums, as well as "sharing" on a Facebook wall or Twitter, further drives this interaction, while bringing potential customers in on the conversation.

Dynamic Content

I can't stress enough how important good storytelling is. Dynamic content will help you encourage people to come back. The more often they come, the more often you'll have an opportunity for them to see your call to action...you know, the thing you want them to do on your website so that you can make money.

Web Standards

Generally, when we talk about Web standards, we are talking about coding. I'd like to address it in a much broader sense here. The way people expect your website to function is important. For example, it is generally accepted that the logo is at the top left and a contact button is at the top right and/or in the footer. The way people naturally react based on past experience is what I call a Web standard. When you deviate from these standards, you run the risk of confusing a visitor. And, a confused visitor is less likely to respond to your call to action.

CONVERSION RATE OPTIMIZATION (CRO)

Now, we get at the heart of the importance of usability. It's one thing to have your website set up so that people know what to do, but it is something entirely more complicated to optimize it so that most of them do what you want them do to.

CRO – AKA Conversion Rate Optimization – Creating the optimal conditions on your Web site to accomplish the objective of your Web page. Whether it is making a sale or getting users to sign up for newsletters.

conversion rate optimization

CRO

CRO BAR

Will marketing help me reach my ideal customer?

Marketing will always help you reach your ideal customer. The real question should be, will online marketing help me reach my ideal customer. The answer to that is, maybe. You have to think of your primary objective and then identify which strategies will help you reach your goal. If your primary audience is not online, the online marketing is a waste of money and effort.

This is where conversion rate optimization (CRO) comes into play. We've talked about conversions as visitors doing what you want them to on your site. It could be clicking on another page, filling out a form or buying a product. Every time you get a customer to do something you want, it's another conversion. The conversion rate is the percentage of people that do what you want versus the number of people that don't.

So, in simplest terms, CRO is making a website so easy to use that the most number of people do what you want them to. Each step of the process should be so well defined that no one has to guess.

> Like all forms of design, visual design is about problem solving, not about personal preference or unsupported opinion.
> – Bob Baxley

Let's talk about a few key tactics to help with conversion rate optimization.

Client Surveys

You hopefully have a current set of clients that at least like you a little bit. Why not send them a simple survey? You don't have to make it complicated. In fact, you'll want to make sure that you don't ask too many questions or they'll tune out. I recommend that there are only three questions that you even need to ask them:

- What is one thing you love about our website?
- What is one thing you'd love to see improved about our website?
- Would you feel comfortable recommending a friend to use our website?

After you gather the information, examine it thoroughly and implement the feedback that best helps you achieve your objectives.

> Trying to increase sales simply by driving more traffic to a website with a poor customer conversion rate is like trying to keep a leaky bucket full by adding more water instead of plugging the holes.
> – Bryan Eisenberg

Five-Second Test

A five-second test is probably one of the easiest ways to get quick feedback, and there are online services that can conduct these tests for you. The idea with a five-second test is that people see an image of your homepage or key landing page for only five seconds. Then, they are asked a series of questions to see what they remember about the design. The more they get wrong, the more you know you have to change. Here are some sample questions you could consider:

- What is the name of the company?
- What does this company do?
- What services does this company offer?
- Are you interested in learning more about this company?

You'll want to be sure that those taking the five-second test have never seen your website before. It is also best if they don't even know your company at all. However, you may have a different set of questions for people that know who you are but haven't seen your new website design yet, such as:

- What is the primary product/service that we are focusing on?
- What do we want you to do on the website?
- Does it make you want to learn more?

A /B Testing

Testing different versions of your website is a good way to get to know what people might do. The problem with five-second tests is that people will often say one thing and do something different. So, it actually has to be tested in real life.

A/B testing is sometimes called spit testing. The concept here is that a certain percentage of users will see a variation of your homepage or landing page, allowing you to measure what they do with the different versions.

To understand better the concept of A/B testing, let's use an analogy of handing out fliers at a large event such as a county fair. The person handing out the fliers has a stack of two different types of fliers, which are variations of the same message. They each have a discount code on them so that performance can be tracked. They're passed out to everyone of every socio-economic background, religion and age group. As people respond using the unique coupon code, we get a better sense of which design has a greater impact. We can then judge conversion rates, because we'll know how many we passed out versus how many took action.

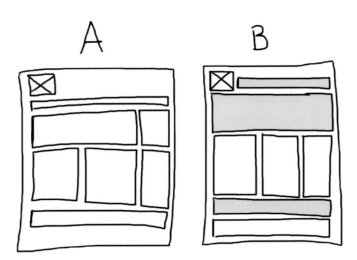

Should we set the standard for our industry?

Setting the standard by which others judge is always a good thing for a brand. It is a point of true differentiation. It allows a competitive distinction and an opportunity within your industry to be sought after for your guidance.

But, you might be wondering, "What if our industry doesn't use the Web?"

This puts you in a very strong position. First, you don't have industry standards you have to conform to that cost money. Second, you have the ability to define how everyone else will do things. Third, you have the ability to wow your customers and set a new status quo.

A/B testing for your own website is similar to the fliers at the fair. When you have a test that you want to perform, you'll present, at random, different versions of your home page or other landing page to your visitors and test their performance. This will require your designers to create alternate pages and your technical talent to create the tests so that you can analyze performance.

Focus Groups

By far, my favorite way to test the usability and conversion rate of a website is by having focus groups. I think that a more appropriate way of doing a focus group is to actually have a focus person. A focus group is sitting with a number of people and trying to discern what they all are doing. When you take this one-on-one with a focus person, you have an opportunity to really understand what they are doing and how they feel about the website's performance.

When you are testing how a website functions, the process is very simple. You'll sit down one-on-one with an individual that is in your target audience, and you'll give them tasks to accomplish on your website. These will be simple tasks that the average person would normally do such as, "I'd like you to tell me how the pricing of my services works." Another simple task could be, "Go to my contact form and ask for more information."

When you do a focus study, like with the five-second test, you'll want to make sure that the person has not used your website before and that he or she is a good representation of your target audience.

> It's really hard to design products by focus groups. A lot of times, people don't know what they want until you show it to them.
> – Steve Jobs

BRINGING IT ALL TOGETHER

Good design doesn't happen by accident. Great marketing isn't something that occurs overnight. It takes time, testing and a willingness to change.

I recognize that change is hard. If you really want to effectively market your business online, you'll need to take the time to go through the three key marketing elements of the Foundational Approach to Web Marketing: SEO, traffic and CRO.

As you go through the process of testing your website, you have to be willing to make the suggested changes. It's a chance to swallow your pride and make your site better.

Sometimes it's hard to recognize that something needs to be changed. I heard a story about engineers from HP that were watching behind a glass as end users tried to install a printer on a computer. They found that, when the users couldn't follow the instructions, they wanted to yell through the glass, "It's right there!"

Thinking back to the American propaganda of World War II, it's easy to see how all marketing works together. In looking at just one of the tactics—posters—many of the elements of online marketing still fit. The content was spectacular and told great stories. The message was distributed by friends, companies, mail and magazines, among other methods. There were multiple versions of the posters, and the ones that generated the most action were the ones that were used most often.

Your organization's marketing should be no different. Each element of the message must be crafted, delivered and tested. Then, you need to start over and do it again for ongoing success. The most important concept to take out of this idea that "change is hard" is that you cannot rely on your marketing endeavors of the past to take you where you want to go in the future. To stay

> *Death by Meeting* by Patrick Lencioni – As a CEO, you need to know the best ways to maximize productivity within meetings. This book will help you lead more meaningful and productive meetings.

fresh in marketing means to try new things and not get stuck in your ways. If your marketing becomes stale, more likely than not your brand will too.

Your organization's marketing should be no different, and you shouldn't be afraid of change. As a CEO, you should not be afraid of change. You must always be open to new things, even if you can't initially see the need for it.

WRAPPING IT UP

On July 7, 2004, a virtually unknown U.S. Senate candidate from Illinois gave the keynote address at the Democratic National Convention. The speech left Democrats inspired and Republicans unsure of what they were in for.

Less than three years later, on February 10, 2007, then Senator Obama announced his candidacy for president of the United States for the 2008 election. Democrats and Republicans alike assumed there was no way that an unknown junior senator from Illinois was going to have a hope winning the primary bid for the Democratic party, let alone become the next president.

So, how was this no-name senator elected to the highest office in the country? The answer is simple: online marketing.

The traditional approach to most political campaigns includes billboard, television, radio and magazine advertisements. Of course, don't forget the signs that are put in front yards across the country and the ever-popular bumper stickers.

But the Barack Obama campaign did things differently. Of course, he still used many of these traditional approaches, but the most effective

> We are lonesome animals. We spend all our life trying to be less lonesome. One of our ancient methods is to tell a story begging the listener to say -- and to feel -- Yes, that's the way it is, or at least that's the way I feel it. You're not as alone as you thought.
> – John Steinbeck

marketing strategy for the Obama primary bid and, later, the Obama-Biden ticket in 2008 was the effective and generous use of online marketing.

Campaign organizers knew that there was no single approach that was the silver bullet; rather, they focused on a fully integrated approach to online marketing. Obama's team built a spectacular Web presence that was focused on his one, primary objective of getting elected, and all of the elements of the Foundational Approach to Web Marketing were present in his campaign. Through effective use of content and graphics, he was able to tell a story that compelled people to action by changing their hearts and minds.

Using Google as an indicator of a successful (or not so successful) online presence, let's look at the 2008 online stats of Senators Obama and McCain. As of November 2008, Senator Obama had over 1.8 million pages in the Google index, and Senator McCain had less than 31,000 pages. This disparity speaks directly to Obama's success in search engine optimization and highlights what successful online marketing can accomplish. The content that was written by his team and others provided search engines with plenty of fodder, the campaign website's code was impeccable and the compelling nature of the site's content encouraged others to provide inbound links. Recall, inbound links tell Google and other search engines that a site is valuable or useful.

More importantly, the Obama campaign didn't limit itself to only a website. The team utilized multiple websites and social media venues, providing potential voters with several ways to engage in the campaign. In fact, the single most visible online strategy that Barack Obama engaged in was social media marketing. This was at the heart of his traffic generation strategy, and it was so effective that it allowed others to talk about him and share his vision with family and friends.

In examining the use of social media in the 2008 presidential campaign, there are some significant comparisons between Senator Obama and Senator McCain. For example, as of November 2008, the Obama campaign had over 495,000 Facebook wall posts and the McCain campaign had less than 133,000. Similarly, Obama's Twitter account had over 115,000 followers and McCain had less than 5,000.

Prior to receiving the Democratic presidential nomination, Obama also used email marketing very effectively as a traffic generator by sending requests to his core followers to help his campaign. In February 2008 during the primary election bid, for example, Hillary Clinton became very concerned about her campaign performance and, in light of Obama's fundraising capability, she loaned her campaign $5 million of her own money. The Obama campaign sent an email to their distribution list and, within 24 hours, they received $8 million in new donations.

Perhaps the least visible tactic the Obama campaign utilized was conversion rate optimization. When visitors arrived at the campaign website's homepage, they were met with a variety of different presentations, which were designed to help the campaign determine which fundraising tactics were the most effective. Some visitors were met with variances as simple as a different word or two in the page's copy, and others saw a completely different picture or even a different way a simple form was presented. These changes weren't limited to the homepage but were also utilized in key areas of the campaign site as well. By analyzing which tactics were the most effective, campaign managers were able to increase fundraising, effectively helping Obama achieve his primary objective of becoming the 44th president of the United States of America.

Just like in Obama's campaign, adherence to the Foundational Approach to Web Marketing leads to successful online marketing efforts. It's not merely a set of tactics but, rather, a way to plan for how everything will work together. By starting with a

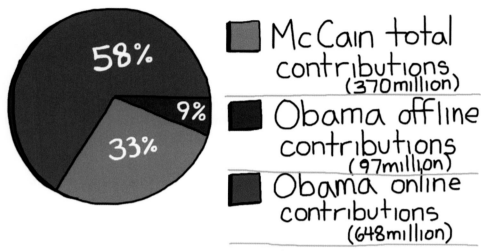

2008 Presidential Race

- 58%
- 9%
- 33%

■ McCain total contributions, (370million)

■ Obama offline contributions (97million)

■ Obama online contributions (648million)

✳ 87% of all Obama donations were online

During the 2008 presidential election, the Obama-Biden ticket generated $648 million through online marketing efforts. In other words, 58% of all campaign donations between the Obama-Biden and McCain-Palin tickets were gener-ated online by the Obama-Biden ticket using the principles of the Foundational Approach to Web Marketing.

strong foundation, known as your Web presence, and building upon that with search engine optimization, traffic generation and conversion rate optimization, you'll realize the greatest level of success in your Web marketing efforts. In doing so, you'll take your company to the next level and capitalize on the quickly growing venue of online marketing.

By using the Foundational Approach to Web Marketing, you can effectively enhance your brand awareness, drive traffic to your Web presence and optimize customer behavior. You'll reach customers and clients that you may have never reached before, and you'll find new and creative ways to engage them. Using this book as your guide, take the steps toward creating a meaningful Web presence that utilizes the strategies and principles of effective online marketing.

REFERENCES

If you would like to learn more, check out these resources

Vin Fiz:

- http://www.drinkvinfiz.com/
- http://www.census.gov/hhes/www/income/data/historical/household/index.html

Disney:

- http://www.justdisney.com/walt_disney/biography/w_disneyland.html
- http://www.disneydreamer.com/history/disneyland.htm
- http://www.yesterland.com/1966brochure.html

Propaganda:

- http://www.webcrawlerblog.com/history/us-propaganda-during-world-war-ii
- http://library.thinkquest.org/C0111500/ww2/american/amerprop.htm
- http://en.wikipedia.org/wiki/Propaganda
- http://en.wikipedia.org/wiki/American_propaganda_during_World_War_II
- http://en.wikipedia.org/wiki/Joseph_Goebbels
- http://en.wikipedia.org/wiki/Adolf_Hitler

Obama:

- http://www.barack-obama-timeline.com/
- http://money.cnn.com/2008/02/29/technology/leonard_politics.fortune/
- http://www.dwsmg.com/barack-obama-marketing-guide.html
- http://history.howstuffworks.com/american-history/barack-obama9.htm
- http://www.widerfunnel.com/about/media/obamas-online-lessons-for-marketers
- http://www.schoonzie.com/barack-obama-is-running-google-website-optimizer
- http://adultaddstrengths.com/2008/11/05/obama-vs-mccain-social-media/

Internet Stats:

- http://www.marketingsherpa.com
- http://searchenginewatch.com
- http://pewinternet.org/

Acknowledgements

I am sure that I'll miss most of the people that have made this book possible. So, I'll leave last names out and hopefully you think it's about you when you see your name.

Andy: Fonts and typography may not be important to me but without your expertise, this book would have been written in my hand.

Don: I heart your illustration talents. Without your artwork this book could never have been a realization of my vision.

Sean: Thank you for taking care of the clean up of my sloppy writing.

Maryanna & Kelly: Without Aloha Publishing, I am not sure I'd have gotten beyond the first page.

Tribute Media Team: Each of you have put up with my ranting and shifting priorities to make my dreams your reality

Jared & Nick: Even though you are off to see your own riches now, you helped to develop the seed of the Foundational Approach to Web Marketing.

Stacy: Thanks for your invaluable feedback in the editing of this book.

Staycee: Your encouragement and willingness to dish out as well as you take it make projects like this worth it.

Justin: You have been a bigger part of my success than most realize. Your guidance in my business and for this book have been invaluable.

Dad: Thank you for teaching me the value of hard work. I may not always agree with your opinions, but I always value them.

Should your website be
RANKED
or TANKED?

How does your website compete? A powerful web presence is vital to expanding your business. Does your website give you the advantage you deserve? Take the self assessment at rankortank.com to find out now!

Corey Smith

You know, I have a varied past. Well, a really varied past. Usually, when you think of someone that runs a Web firm, you think of either a coder or a graphics guy.

Well, I am neither.

At 16, I ran an offset printing press for my father.

At 21, after a mission for my church in Albania, I bought and sold printing and graphics services. I taught myself how to use my $400 Macintosh to produce graphics that I could sell.

Website: **coreysmith.ws**
Twitter: **@corey_smith**
Facebook: **facebook.com/Corey.Allyn.Smith**
About Me: **about.me/coreysmith**
Email: **smith@coreysmith.ws**

IKON Office Solutions actually hired me to use my self-taught graphics skills to run a graphics department for them in Salt Lake City in 1998... the same year I married my beautiful bride, Jennifer.

Together, Jen and I have five wonderful children... yeah... full house.

I have always had a passion for business, technology and education. So, after working in the office equipment industry for over 8 years, teaching graphic design for Web at the University of Utah, serving as a Color Systems Specialist for Canon USA, working hard to learn what I could, and going back to school for my undergraduate in Information Technology and a Master in Business Administration, both from University of Phoenix, I started Tribute Media in 2007.

During the years since starting Tribute Media, I've worked hard to develop talents that can be shared with others. I figure that a talent that can't be shared isn't a talent worth having. I believe that this book is one example of how I can share what I've learned.